PRIMITIVE PIETY REVIVED,

OR

THE AGGRESSIVE POWER OF THE CHRISTIAN CHURCH.

A

PREMIUM ESSAY.

BY

REV. HENRY C. FISH,
NEWARK, N. J.

BOSTON:
CONGREGATIONAL BOARD OF PUBLICATION,
16 TREMONT TEMPLE.
1855.

CAMBRIDGE:
ALLEN AND FARNHAM, STEREOTYPERS AND PRINTERS.

PREMIUM OFFERED.

A benevolent individual, deeply impressed with the importance of a more elevated type of piety in the churches and in the ministry, placed at the disposal of the Congregational Board of Publication the sum of two hundred dollars, to be given to the author of the best Essay on

The more perfect exemplification in Christian life of the doctrines of the gospel, and with special reference to the conversion of sinners to Christ. Particularly: —

To set forth in a just and striking light, the grand defects of Christian character which hinder the triumph of the Redeemer's kingdom on earth, and the *cause* of these defects:

To delineate the true New Testament model of Christian character and Christian life:

To revive and perpetuate the faith illustrated in the eleventh chapter of Hebrews, as an energizing and all-conquering *principle*, actually subordinating earthly things to heavenly:

To show the true sense of the self-denial required by Christ as essential to discipleship:

To urge the peculiar responsibility of Christians at the present day, to attain to a higher degree of faith and holiness, and to exhibit the same, particularly in personal efforts for the salvation of men: Together with

The motives and means of this attainment.

The Committee of Examination and Award are Dr. Humphrey of Pittsfield, Dr. Ide of West Medway, and Dr. Hawes of Hartford.

PREMIUM AWARDED.

THE Committee appointed to receive and pass upon the merits of manuscripts for a Premium Essay on the above-named subject, have examined all the manuscripts put into their hands, and award the premium to REV. HENRY C. FISH of Newark, N. J., author of the one entitled PRIMITIVE PIETY REVIVED, or THE AGGRESSIVE POWER OF THE CHRISTIAN CHURCH, as upon the whole the best.

Several others are well written, and two or three are of such decided merit that the Committee would be glad to see them in print.

H. HUMPHREY,
J. IDE,
J. HAWES.

" The church itself requires conversion." — *Harris.*

" The great want of this age, is the regeneration of Christendom." — *Baird.*

" To the Great Head of the Church we must look for a new order of men, — men just as absorbed in winning souls to Christ, as worldlings are in gathering gold." — *Kincaid.*

TO

THE GENEROUS FRIEND,

WITH WHOSE LIBERALITY THIS ESSAY ORIGINATED;

TO THE AUTHOR'S PIOUS AND VENERABLE PARENTS;

AND TO ALL WHO DESIRE A REVIVAL OF THE PRIMITIVE FAITH IN THE CHURCHES OF OUR LORD JESUS CHRIST;

THESE PAGES

ARE AFFECTIONATELY INSCRIBED.

CONTENTS.

CHAPTER I.

AN INQUIRY AS TO THE ACTUAL EXISTENCE OF ANY SERIOUS DEFECTS IN THE PREVAILING PIETY OF THE AGE.

CHAPTER II.

FIRST GRAND DEFECT OF THE PREVAILING PIETY OF THE TIMES — A WANT OF SIMPLICITY OF PURPOSE.

CHAPTER III.

CHAPTER IV.

CHAPTER V.

THE WANT OF A SCRIPTURAL FAITH — A GRAND DEFECT IN THE PREVAILING TYPE OF PIETY.

CHAPTER VI.

FIFTH GRAND DEFECT — A WANT OF EARNESTNESS.

CHAPTER VII.

SIXTH GRAND DEFECT — WANT OF INDIVIDUALISM.

CHAPTER VIII.

THE GRAND REMEDY FOR ALL EXISTING DEFECTS IN CHRISTIAN CHARACTER — A GENERAL AND POWERFUL REVIVAL OF RELIGION IN THE CHURCHES.

PRIMITIVE PIETY REVIVED.

CHAPTER I.

AN INQUIRY AS TO THE ACTUAL EXISTENCE OF ANY SERIOUS DEFECTS IN THE PREVAILING PIETY OF THE AGE.

The Fiery Cross. — The Great Usurpation. — The promised Messiah. — The Mission of His Followers. — The Injunction not regarded. — Present Condition of the Church of Christ: much to commend; much to lament. — The Type of Piety. — Proofs of its Defectiveness. — General Opinion. — Ministerial Destitution. — Unconcern for the Heathen. — Progress of the Mission Work. — Missionary Pictures of the Bible. — Counterpart not found. — Not to be attributed to Pecuniary Inability. — Wealth of United States Christians. — Not attributable to want of Numerical Force. — Primitive Disciples. — Third Proof: Small Success of Gospel in Christian Lands. — Proportion of Inhabitants pious. — Relative increase of Christians and United States Population. — Facts as to New York City. — Home Heathen. — Inevitable Conclusion. — Objections answered. — Outward Appearances deceptive. — Organism not Power. — Zion to put on her Strength.

THAT was a beautiful custom of the ancient Scottish chiefs, the assembling of their clans by means of the herald and the Fiery Cross. In the event of any invasion upon his territory, or any sudden emergency, the chieftain slew a goat; and the priest, making a cross of light wood, and scathing it with fire, and quenching the flaming points in the blood

1

of the animal, held it aloft, and cried in substance, thus:—

> "When flits this cross from man to man,
> Vich-Alpine's summons to his clan,
> Burst be the ear that fails to heed!
> Palsied the foot that shuns to speed!"

The chieftain, then receiving the cross, delivered it to a swift and trusty messenger, who was to run at full speed to the next hamlet, and present it to a principal person, with a simple word, implying the place of rendezvous. He who received the symbol, considered himself solemnly bound, under the most fearful anathemas, to send it forward with the same despatch to the next village, until it should have passed through all the country which owed allegiance to the chief. And, at its appearance, every ablebodied man from sixteen years old to sixty, was to repair, with the least possible delay, to the designated place.

How inspiring the scene! Forth plunges the messenger of "blood and brand," in his fleet career. Parched are his burning lips and brow, but by the fountain he pauses not. He breasts the cragged hill, he springs across the "trembling bog and false morass," nor fails till he has delivered the symbol to a second messenger, who transmits it with equal haste to a third, and thus the Fiery Cross glanced "like a meteor round."

The huts and hamlets are in arms; and hardy men are poured from highland and glen. The fisherman forsakes his nets; the smith his anvil; the herdsman his flock;—the mower drops his scythe in the half-cut swath — the plough in mid-furrow stays, and every loyal son presses to stand in arms by his chieftain's side.

The empire of *our* KING has been invaded. Never did a sovereign hold possession by a more righteous title; for he created the world and all things that are therein. But for this, Satan, his great rival, was not the less desirous of supplanting and superseding him.

In his cunning craftiness he planned a revolt. It was too successful. He established his kingdom, and thought to hold on earth an undisputed sway. But God in mercy to man had otherwise determined. Upon the heel of the revolt had followed the threat of his final defeat. The seed of the woman should bruise the serpent's head. In due time, that "seed" appeared to execute the threatening, and destroy the works of the devil. Having laid deep and broad the foundation of an everlasting kingdom, the Messiah permitted himself to fall into the hands of wicked men, and was crucified and slain. Possessing, however, the power of laying down his life, he had power to take it up again. Rising from the tomb, and ascending up on high, he commissioned his followers to coöperate in bringing a revolted world into allegiance with its rightful Lord and King. Lifting high the blood-stained cross, the heralds of salvation were to go into all the world, and "make ready a people prepared for the Lord." How far have they been faithful to their trust? And where the cross has appeared, to what extent have men allied themselves to the interests of our King? Alas, that those to whom the gospel has been given, with the charge to send it forward to others, have been so negligent of their duty! Alas, that the oppressed subjects of the "prince of this world," have been so reluctant to come up to the help of the Lord against the mighty!

But what is the present condition and actual progress of the Christian Church? Than this there cannot be a question of greater importance. It relates to every thing that is dear to Christ, and essential to the highest interests of man.

Upon a careful survey of the churches, as they now present themselves, there is much to rejoice and encourage the pious heart. Their numerous membership embraces a fair proportion of the intelligence, and wealth, and influence of the land; and between the different religious denominations there exists a good degree of fraternal sympathy and affection. Their kindly influences are constantly extending themselves. The discoveries and applications in the department of science, united with commerce — one of God's great agents — and the spirit of inquiry which prompts the researches of the scholar and the antiquarian, have opened up the most distant and obscure parts of the globe, and placed in communication with each other the different nations, thereby diffusing somewhat of Christian influence.

More prominent are the direct religious forces operating through their missionaries and mission churches, and the multiplied copies of the Scriptures, for the evangelization of the heathen. Wonderful, indeed, has been the change in public sentiment upon the subject of missions, since the days when Sidney Smith publicly ridiculed the idea that a man, whom he styled, by way of contempt, the "consecrated cobbler," should trouble his mind, and the minds of others, about the conversion of four hundred and twenty millions of pagans, — a project which appeared not more chimerical to him, than to nine tenths of the then existing population of Christendom. And wonderful the advance in outward Christian benevolence, since that germinal missionary collection of twelve pounds, thirteen shillings, and sixpence, at a meeting in Kettering in the year 1792. But notwithstanding these encouraging considerations, it must be acknowledged that there is much in the present condition of the Christian Church to chasten our rejoicings, awaken our concern, and impel us to earnest prayer and deep contrition before God.

In the opinion of many there is cause for the deepest solicitude in regard to the *type of piety* that now generally prevails. The following language of a benevolent individual, is a fair expression of this sentiment: "As compared with the work now demanded by the exigencies of Christ's kingdom, the present is an age of worldliness, of lukewarmness, and self-indulgence. The merest modicum, as a general thing, is given to the work of Christ, while multitudes go for fashion, extravagance, and luxury. Even the little we do for foreign missions seems in danger of bribing our consciences into the neglect of the perishing around us. The broad way is still the thronged way." *

* The unknown author of the proposal, which was the more immediate occasion of the preparation of this Essay

The very grave question which it is proposed now to consider, relates to the justness of this opinion. It may be thus concisely stated: *Is the prevailing piety of the present age seriously defective?* Let us not shrink from the honest investigation of this subject. Let the Church of Christ consider that her strength and beauty are in exact proportion to her true piety; and that of whatever else she may boast, it is but the "earthly attire which she will throw off, as she steps across the threshold of eternity, to enter the temple of God." Let her thoroughly examine her condition, and in doing it, devoutly pray: "Search me, O God, and know my heart; try me, and know my thoughts: and see if there be any wicked way in me, and lead me in the way everlasting."

The opinion of enlightened and pious men, already alluded to, is of importance in attaining to a just conclusion upon the question at issue. It is not less remarkable for its prevalence than for its obvious credibility. The number of such as reverence antiquity, and decry every thing that belongs to the present, is always great; as is also that of individuals whose views are adopted without careful and impartial examination. Hence a *prevalent* is not always a *just* opinion. But upon this subject there comes to us testimony from those whose judgment, and facilities for observation, are such, as to entitle their views to the highest consideration. Says the Rev. John Angell James, speaking of the spiritual condition of the great body of the professors of religion: "Amidst much that is cheering, there is, on the other hand, much that is discouraging and distressing to the more pious observer. We behold a strange combination of zeal and worldly-mindedness; great activity for the extension of religion in the earth, united with lamentable indifference to the state of religion in the soul; in short, apparent vigor in the extremities, with a growing torpor at the heart. Multitudes are substituting zeal for piety, liberality for mortification, and a social for a personal religion. No careful reader of the New Testament, and observer of the present state of the church, can fail to be convinced, one should think, that what is now wanting is a high spirituality. The Christian profession is sinking in its tone of piety; the line of separation between the church and the world becomes less and less perceptible; and the character of genuine Christianity, as expounded from pulpits and delineated in books, has too rare a counterpart in the lives and spirit of its professors."*

In a late discourse upon the Apostolic Ministry, a distinguished American divine held the following language upon the same subject: "But what is the condition of our churches of all denominations at this critical moment? The disciples of Christ seem to be fast losing the distinctive marks of their profession. Self-denial for the cause of the Redeemer will soon become the exception rather than the rule. In large districts of the country, the admissions to the churches are not as numerous as the removals by death. In the mean time the number of candidates for the ministry is diminishing in all denominations, not only relatively but absolutely. Nay, it is

* Earnest Ministry, p. 62, 63.

diminishing more rapidly than the figures indicate, for of the reputed number of candidates a considerable portion never enter the ministry; and of those who enter it, a greater and greater number leave it for other pursuits." *

The language here cited, it will be perceived, represents different religious denominations, and different hemispheres, and may be taken as specimens of what might be extensively adduced.

This prevailing belief in the general decline of primitive piety, is confirmed by the *inadequate supply of Christian ministers*, referred to in the above. It is an observation of Isaac Taylor, "that a religious body, within which there is vitality, will ordinarily supply itself with an adequate proportion of ministers." Beyond question there is truth in this language of that able and sagacious writer.

The young convert to Christianity naturally takes upon himself the type of piety borne by the church into which he is introduced. If that is highly spiritual, he remains spiritually minded; if the reverse, he will almost surely sink to the same low level. Now it is the measure of holy love in the soul that determines, to some extent, the question of consecrating one's self to the work of the ministry.† If the deep principles and strong emotions of a truly devoted soul obtain, the individual will find it exceedingly difficult, if not impossible, to resist the call of God to preach the gospel. A woe, ringing in his

* Rev. F. Wayland, D. D., Discourse, p. 78.

† For "the ministerial spirit is only the *Christian* spirit, under a peculiar form and with a peculiar direction."

ears, a fire, shut up in his bones, will forbid his resting satisfied with any other pursuit than that of the ministry of reconciliation. A stream that is full and rapid in its current, is not readily diverted from the deepened channel. And so if there were depth and force in the piety of our young men, neither the attractions of worldly pursuits on the one hand, nor the discouragements of the ministry on the other, could turn them from the path of duty. Moreover, when the piety of the churches is what it ought to be, there will be much and earnest *prayer* for laborers in the Lord's harvest; and also a diligent watching and searching for the gifts that God may bestow; as well as liberal provision and encouragement for those who meet with difficulties in qualifying themselves for the work to which they are called. It is, therefore, true that if there be vitality in the church there will not long exist any serious deficiency in the number of good ministers of Jesus Christ.

What, then, judged by this standard, must be the character of the prevailing piety of the times upon which we have fallen? If there is a single fact universally admitted and deplored, it is that of an alarming destitution as regards preachers of the gospel. It is stated, though the estimate may be somewhat too high, that in one denomination there are four thousand more churches than available ministers; while from every branch of the Christian Church, and every quarter of the globe comes the cry, "Send us men to thrust in the sickle; the harvest is plenteous, but the laborers are few."

That many causes, such as the inadequate support of the ministry, the difficulties of a thorough mental preparation, the accumulating labors and responsibilities of the sacred office, and the like, have operated to produce this lamentable destitution, is unquestionably true; but the cause is more remote than all this. It may be traced back to the character of the piety that generally prevails in the churches. Speculate as we may, the root of the whole difficulty lies precisely here.

Prescribe remedies as we may, there can be no remedy that will prove efficacious, which is not applied here. A vital, scriptural piety will produce an adequate ministry: but the Christian Church has not an adequate ministry; therefore has she not a scriptural piety.

An estimate of the prevailing piety of the age, may be formed from an examination of *the character and extent of Christian effort for evangelizing the nations.*

The church of Christ is essentially aggressive. The great command of its founder is, "Go, disciple all nations." If the piety of the church conform to the divine standard, the obligation of this command will be acknowledged and felt. If we love Christ as we ought, we shall keep His commandments. If we love our neighbor as ourselves, we shall not look upon his misery with an unfeeling heart, and pass by on the other side. True piety will induce action. Faith without works is dead.

With these admitted principles in view, we inquire as to the nature and extent of the past and present efforts to disseminate the knowledge of the true God. It is now about sixty years since the modern missionary movement began. And, although its achievements have been surpassingly sublime, little has been accomplished, compared with what yet remains to be done.

If we turn to the volume of Divine truth, how glowing its descriptions of the ultimate triumphs of the truth! How bright its missionary pictures! " The kingdoms of this world shall become the kingdoms of our Lord, and of his Christ." " Ask of me and I will give thee the heathen for thine inheritance and the uttermost parts of the earth for thy possession." " I will gather all nations and tongues, and cause them to come and see my glory." " From the rising of the sun, even to the going down of the same, my name shall be great among the Gentiles; and in every place shall incense be offered to my name, and a pure offering." " The mountain of the Lord's house shall be established in the top of the mountains, and shall be exalted among the hills, and all nations shall flow unto it." " Ethiopia shall stretch forth her hands unto God." " The isles shall wait for his law." " All nations shall call him blessed." " The wilderness and the solitary place shall be glad for them, and the desert shall rejoice and blossom as the rose. It shall blossom abundantly, and rejoice even with joy and singing." " At the name of Jesus every knee shall bow, and every tongue confess that he is Christ to the glory of God the Father." " For the earth shall be filled with the knowledge of the glory of the Lord, as the waters cover the sea."

The time is to come when the earth shall present the counterpart of these bright pictures; when from every spot on its surface, pure offerings shall ascend in one continuous stream; and our globe, "as it rolls along its orbit, shall seem but a censor revolving in the hand of the great High-Priest, and pouring out at every aperture a cloud, dense and rich, of incense, fragrant and grateful to God."

But how painful the contrast between what the world is *to be* and what it *is!*

According to the most reliable estimates, our globe is peopled by *one thousand millions* of human beings. Two thirds of these, or about seven hundred millions, are pagans, Mohammedans, and Jews; of the latter there being only about six millions, and of the Mohammedans one hundred millions. The remaining three hundred millions are called *Christians* in distinction from those above named. But of these about two hundred millions are Romanists,* while some fifty millions belong to the Greek Church; either of which classes can be considered Christians only in *name;* since, whatever may be said of occasional exceptions, as a mass, they practically conform but too closely, in religious matters, to the inhabitants of heathen lands.

The number of Protestants in the world is estimated at seventy millions; which includes many sects and classes in whom, it is feared, exists but little of vital godliness. Eighteen years since, accepting the calculation of Dr. Samuel Miller,† only about one third of the Protestant population of the world

---

* The estimate of the Pope of Rome is here assumed, although it is difficult to perceive how it can be sustained. See Baird's Christian Register, 1850.

† See his Serm. at 26th Ann. of A. B. C. F. Missions.

had the true gospel preached among them in any thing like its purity. Only one half of that part called evangelical, were even *professors* of religion, in any distinct or intelligent import of the terms.

Admitting the relative proportion to have remained substantially the same, there are now existing in the world, upon this estimate, but about *twelve millions* who make any intelligent profession of piety. What proportion of these can justly claim to be truly pious, is known to God alone. But saying nothing of this, is not the spectacle that presents itself truly appalling? *Six hundred millions of human beings* lying in the cold, dark, death-damps of heathenism, and soon to go down to the darker chambers of death!

Two hundred millions, blindly adhering to a most fatal system, where "science and ignorance, refinement and barbarism, wisdom and stupidity, taste and animalism, mistaken zeal and malignant enmity, may sanctimoniously pour out their virulence against the gospel, and cry, Hosannah, while they go forth to shed the blood, and to wear out the patience of the saints!" *One hundred millions* deluded by that fell imposture, that lifts up the crescent where stood the cross, and sheds its blight upon the once fairest and most favored portions of the earth, and millions of others who have the *form* of godliness, but are wholly destitute of its *power!*

And this in the last half of the nineteenth century of the Christian era! Was it strange that the Karen inquirer should ask of the missionary, "If so long time has elapsed since the crucifixion of Christ, why has not this good news reached us before? Why have

2

so many generations of our fathers gone down to hell for want of it?" May it not be a matter of astonishment to the angels, who might covet the privilege of heralding the good tidings to all the dwellers on the earth, as of old to the few shepherds upon the plains of Bethlehem? Had they been commissioned to the glorious service, how quickly had they sped on silver wings, until they had compassed the globe, shouting on their gladsome way, "Glory to God in the highest, and on earth peace, good-will toward men!"

But how shall we account for the fact, that, after eighteen centuries have passed away, the larger proportion of the world remains covered with pagan darkness? How is it, that although it is now sixty years since the commencement of the modern missionary movement, the mass of the human race is unvisited by the heralds of salvation? The cause cannot be found in any supposed pecuniary inability on the part of the Christian church.

The entire sum of money contributed annually by the churches of Great Britain for foreign missionary purposes, is about two millions of dollars; the contributions of the American churches, of all denominations, for like purposes, do not exceed eight hundred thousand dollars. Aggregate contributions from Great Britain and America, not far from $2,800,000.

But let us confine our attention to American churches. And what an appalling disproportion do we behold, between the wealth and luxury of our country, and the gifts of charity for furnishing to the heathen the word of life! The estimated value of the real and personal estate of the inhabitants of the United States, is $7,133,369,725.* The agricultural products, in four articles alone, in a single year amount to $358,423,323; and the articles produced annually in our manufacturing establishments, (exclusive of such establishments as do not produce to the value of $500,) is $1,020,300,000 annually, with a profit of more than $230,000,000. In these manufactures the sum of $240,000,000 is paid annually for labor. The value of the products of our iron manufactures alone is $54,604,006. The value of gold and silver coined in the United States mint and its branches, amounted in the year 1852, to $57,896,-227, and in 1853, to $64,357,631.

Now it is computed that far more than one half of the wealth and products of this country are in the hands of the friends of religion. Admitting this, how absolutely trifling the sum devoted by the disciples of Christ to the cause of foreign evangelization, when viewed in the light of their real ability! How much more insignificant when placed beside the millions that are given for purposes far less worthy, and, indeed, in some instances, wholly unworthy, and even pernicious. It is stated that more than $1,500,000 are annually expended in the theatres and opera houses of the single city of New York; and that that sum would scarcely cover the cost of the simple article of imported cigars. An English statistician has computed that the laboring classes of Great Britain expend no less than $250,000,000 every year for alcoholic liquors and

* These facts are mostly gathered from the census returns of 1850.

tobacco. The estimate does not include the money spent for the same object, by the middle and upper classes, as they are called.

The entire expense attending the various expeditions in search of Sir John Franklin, is estimated at $3,562,949.

How humiliating the contemplation of facts like these! Twice the whole amount of contributions for foreign missions from American Christians, spent in a single item of useless or sinful indulgence, by the inhabitants of one city! More than *three hundred* times that amount expended in two items of the same nature, by the poorer classes alone of Great Britain; it being nearly *one hundred* times the amount of the united contributions of Christians in England and America! And four times as much money expended in the praiseworthy attempt to rescue a few lost adventurers from temporal death, as all the American Christians, put together, are investing in the enterprise for saving six hundred millions of perishing heathen from eternal perdition!

The annual gifts of Kallee's Temple at Calcutta, are scarcely exceeded in amount by those of all the Christians in America and Great Britain. The benighted pagans devoting for the support of *one heathen temple*, nearly as much as all these professed followers of Jesus are contributing to impart light to those who sit in gross darkness! The contributions of the Jews, both voluntary and prescribed, for the support of their worship, and the relief of their afflicted, exhausted one third of their annual income

If the adherents of a purer faith were, in the same ratio, to consecrate of their substance to the Lord, how few years would elapse before the citadel of Satan were stormed at every point! But, alas, it is *millions* for *Mammon*, and *coppers* for *Christ! Pounds* to *earth*, and *farthings* to *heaven!* Navies and armies, as a devoted missionary of the cross too truly observes, have their millions; railroads and canals have their millions; silks, carpets, and mirrors, have their millions; parties of pleasure, and licentiousness in high life and low life, have their millions: and what has the treasury of God and the Lamb, to redeem a world of souls from the pains of eternal damnation, and to fill them with joys unspeakable? The sum is so small in comparison, that one's tongue refuses to utter it!*

And this has been true, let it be borne in mind, during a period of unprecedented prosperity in every branch of industry and enterprise; when the fields, and the mines, and the shops, and the ships, and the factories, have been rolling in upon their owners the most generous returns for labor and capital; when the discovery of exhaustless deposits of the precious metals has thrown into our lap more than two hundred millions of dollars; when a million of square miles of territory have been added to our domain, when wealthy farmers, and heavy bankers, and extensive manufacturers, and opulent capitalists, and fortunate adventurers, have been rapidly multiplying; and tens of thousands had become rich who but lately, barely met the common necessities of life; when, in short, we were fast becoming the most wealthy, as we are in danger of becoming the most luxurious

* Rev. Sheldon Dibble, Missionary to Sandwich Islands.

nation on the globe; and but for God's restraining grace, and the counteracting influence of charitable claims, were sure of plunging into the gulf of worldliness and folly, which has swallowed up so many nations before us.

The truth is, that Christians are now contributing almost nothing, compared with their real ability. They are scarcely bestowing the crumbs which fall from their tables, for meeting the direst necessities of the poor heathen. Taken as a body, (for there are individual exceptions,) they are giving but a drop from the ocean of their plenty, but a particle from the world of their abundance. The paltry sum of *twenty cents per year* is the *average* of the present contributions from the members of the evangelical churches in the United States for foreign mission purposes. Were they to contribute, severally, the small amount of one dollar per year, (two cents per week,) a sum *greater by a million of dollars* than that now raised by the *entire churches of England and America*, would be secured.

But if the cause of the slow progress of foreign evangelization is not discoverable in the *material*, is it in the *numerical* strength of the Christian church?

Most certainly not; as is obvious, if from no other considerations, from the triumphant progress of Christianity in primitive times. How few were the disciples of our Lord, who, fifty days after his crucifixion, began in earnest to execute their commission, "Go ye into all the world, and preach the gospel to every creature!"

Almost immediately, as the result of the preached word, the one hundred and twenty received an accession of about three thousand souls. We shortly read that they numbered five thousand, and within a year and a half, multitudes had received the truth, "and a great company of the priests were obedient to the faith." "And at that time there was a great persecution against the church which was at Jerusalem, and they were all scattered abroad throughout the regions of Judea and Samaria, except the Apostles."* They went everywhere preaching the word; and in less time than has elapsed since the first modern mission was established in India, that word had been successfully proclaimed throughout all Palestine, and Asia Minor, and Macedonia, and Greece, along the coast of Africa, and in the Islands of the Ægean Sea, in Egypt, and Rome, and, if the traditions of the fathers be accepted on this point, even in India and Spain. Justin, the Martyr, who was beheaded in Rome, A. D. 165, furnishes this remarkable testimony concerning the triumphs of the Christian religion: "There is not a nation, either of Greek, or barbarian, or any other name, even of those who wander in tribes, or live in tents, among whom prayers and thanksgivings are not offered to the Father and Creator of the universe in the name of the crucified Jesus." And Clemens of Alexandria, speaking of the gospel, says, it "is spread through the whole world, in every town and village and city, converting both whole houses and separate individuals." If such results attended the efforts of the few primitive disciples, who had in the main, neither wealth nor learning nor influence; who had

---

* Acts 8: 1.

not the press to bring to their aid; and who were obliged to encounter all kinds and degrees of opposition, what might not have been accomplished by the millions of Christ's followers in our day, had they possessed the same spirit which those early Christians possessed! We are compelled to believe that they have not possessed it, and do not now possess it. And *here* is found the true cause of the surprising delay in sending to all nations the word of eternal life. How painful an evidence of serious defects in the piety of our day!

There is another point in evidence, to the same effect, which cannot now be noticed. It is the *limited success of the gospel in Christian lands.*

A convert from heathenism, on visiting this country and addressing a large assembly, assumed in his remarks that they were all Christians. He was informed of his mistake; and with tearful surprise assured his teacher who accompanied him, that he supposed all the people in America loved the Saviour. He wondered how it was that they did not, since they had all of them so long ago heard of Jesus, and there were so many to teach them the gospel. This, perhaps, was a reasonable expectation; but how wide from the actual reality!

The present population of the United States cannot be less than some twenty-six millions.* The members of churches in connection with the different religious denominations in the country, amount to three million seven hundred and seventy-six thousand

---

* The population in 1850, was 23,198,817. See Census Report.

three hundred and nineteen,* or about one seventh of the whole population. But of these, considering the errors of life and of faith, there can be no doubt, even in the judgment of charity, that very many are only professedly Christians. How small the proportion of those truly converted, even in this highly favored land! And of those who possess not godliness, how many are they who openly oppose all religion, or are the deluded subjects of the "man of sin!" How many portions of our country are yet even unsupplied with the preached gospel!

Not to one part of our land, but to many parts, would apply the language of one who thus writes from a rising State in the north-west: "Romanism is here fortifying his strong-holds, Rationalism is here striving for the mastery, and cold blank Atheism is here, hoping for the realization of its cheerless dreams — a land without her Sabbaths, her ministers, her Bible, or her God." And in deploring the destitution of the means of grace, he says, "There are, in this State, sixty-five thousand children and youth without any religious instruction whatever."

A prominent minister of the gospel recently affirmed that even in Ohio there were fifty towns, with an average population of eight hundred each, almost entirely without any kind of preaching; and two uneducated circuit riders are declared to be the only preachers in a large western county, larger than the entire State of Rhode Island. It is affirmed, on

---

* This estimate is taken from the Presbyterian Almanac for 1854, and is, probably, as accurate as can be obtained. Of course, the Roman Catholics are not included in the estimate.

good authority, that *less than one third* of the population of Ohio, Indiana, Illinois, Missouri, and Iowa is under the direct influence of any evangelical instruction.*

And what shall be said of those parts of the country best supplied with the means of grace? It is not generally known to what an alarming extent those means of grace are disregarded. Even in New England, where the religious element so largely obtains, competent witnesses testify that fully one third of the families neglect the sanctuary.† The state of things in large cities, in this respect, is alarming. A writer in England, of great reputation, says, "The town in which I live contains, with its suburbs, about two hundred and ten thousand inhabitants; and of these, perhaps not more than forty thousand, above twelve years of age, are ever at public worship at the same time." This he states to be but a specimen of other large towns.

It is computed that one million and a half of persons in London do not attend any place of worship, and never hear the sound of the gospel unless it is carried to their doors. From the Census Returns of England in 1851, it appears that probably *four millions* of the people of that country never attend public worship.‡

---

* For several of these facts and others of a similar nature, see a publication of Am. Tract Soc., called "Home Evangelization."

† See "Home Evangelization," p. 26.

‡ Mr. Cobden, in a recent speech at Manchester, stated that this class of persons will now number *five* millions; and that there are a million of *heads of families*, who are not connected with any place of worship whatsoever.

The cities of our own country present facts scarcely less painful to contemplate. A religious paper in New England,* speaking of Concord, N. H., asserts that that city contains a larger proportion of church-going people than the average of its neighboring cities and agricultural towns, but that out of its ten thousand inhabitants, three thousand seldom if ever enter any place of worship on the Sabbath. It believes "that more than one third of her population are without the pale of the saving influence of the gospel."

Statistics carefully prepared have demonstrated that scarcely *one fourth* of the inhabitants of Philadelphia are regular attendants upon any religious services. It is stated, upon the authority of the New York City Tract Society, that there are in that city two hundred thousand persons who are not only not regular, but not even *occasional* attendants upon public worship. This is one third of her whole population. Taking our country as a whole, it is believed by those best qualified to judge, that not far from *one half* of the entire population habitually neglect the sanctuary, or hear "another gospel."

Let us take another view of the subject, and inquire as to the numerical strength of the churches of our land. They are but slowly increasing in numbers. The total membership of all the different denominations in 1844, was about 3,050,950. In the last ten years, therefore, there has been a gain of but about 715,000; which is less than twenty-four per centum. In that time the Roman Catholics have

---

* The Congregational Journal.

increased, in the membership, about *one hundred* per centum; and in the churches and priests, *one hundred and seventy* per centum. Forty years ago they numbered, in this country, but eighty churches and sixty-eight priests; now they report 1,712 churches, 1,574 priests, and a membership of more than 1,732,600, with twenty-five incorporated colleges, and twenty-nine theological seminaries.*

It thus appears that the ratio of increase on the part of Romanists for the last ten years, has been more than than *four times* greater than that of evangelical Christians.

The increase of population in the United States, for the ten years next preceding 1850, was at the rate of about thirty-five per centum. Hence the Roman Catholic ratio of increase, is *sixty-five per cent. greater* than that of the population of the United States, while the comparative *ratio* of evangelical Christians is *eleven per cent. less!*

Descending from this general survey to particular churches and localities, considerations no less humiliating present themselves. Is it not a remarkable fact that many large and wealthy churches are receiving almost no additions, and scarcely repairing, from year to year, the losses which they sustain? Upon an examination of the minutes of an evangelical body in one of our flourishing States, the following statistics of two large churches, the one in the country, the other in a city, are noted: country church, 1843, members, 223; 1853, 198; loss, 25:

---

* These statistics are drawn from the "Metropolitan Catholic Almanac and Laity's Directory." Baltimore, 1854.

city church, 1843, 248; 1853, 221; loss, 27. Turning to the records of another body, and marking the progress of the most prominent church in another large city, it appears that in seven years its membership has increased at the average of one for each year. Now from these three churches, which are selected only as specimens of hundreds in the same condition, no new colonies have been sent out during the terms specified, nor have they encountered any special adverse influences. And yet, with an aggregate of 1,000 members, and appearing in a prosperous condition, they have *actually decreased in the time specified by forty-five members.*

But passing from particular churches, let us examine the statistics of several of the principal evangelical denominations in the "Metropolis of the Union," the city of New York. In 1843, there were of communicants in the O. S. Presbyterian denomination 3,752; in 1853, 4,319; gain in the ten years, 567. Of N. S. Presbyterians in 1843, 7,677; in 1853, 6,770; loss, 907. Of Baptists in 1843, 7,997; in 1853, 8,693; gain, 696. Of Methodist Episcopal in 1843, 9,780; in 1853, 9,319; loss, 461.

Total loss of these denominations in ten years, 105.* And yet the population of New York City

* These statements, however surprising, may be accepted as perfectly reliable. They are based upon the writer's personal and careful investigations. The Reformed Dutch and Protestant Methodist churches are not included because of the difficulty in obtaining accurate statistics. The Congregational churches, so numerous in New England, have sprung up in New York, with one exception, since 1843. Of these, there are now eight churches with a membership of 1,274. — See "*Congregational Year-Book.*"

has doubled itself in those same ten years! Are not such facts absolutely appalling? The population of a mighty city, in the heart of the commonwealth, increasing in so rapid a ratio, and yet evangelical Christians, in point of numbers, *not only not increasing, but scarcely holding their own!* And that, too, when vice is every day more rampant, — when infidelity, among the Germans alone, numbers its 50,000 adherents, — when intemperance is more than a match for the prodigious influence brought to bear against it, — when licentiousness has its 2,500 brothels, and 25,000 abandoned women, — and when a leading religious journal, in allusion to a particular locality in the city, has said of one miserable habitation what might with equal justice be said of hundreds of others: "Every room is swarming. Upon the floor is stretched the young and the old, the black and the white, the sick and the sinning — all in one promiscuous sty! Here the beggar brings his refuse food, and the prowling footpad his spoils, and the poor diseased child of sin her booty purchased by the price of her good name, and ultimately of life itself. Here they grovel; here they drug their consciences in alcoholic poisons; here they linger out their only life on earth; and when the abused and profaned and wretched frame can bear up no longer, *here they die*, and the pauper's grave receives their last loathsome relics! And all this within the sound of a hundred church bells! All this within hail of city schools with their open doors, and of ten thousand Christian homes with their household altars."

How far this description of the state of things in

one city is applicable to others, it is impossible to state. But if the actual and relative progress of evangelical religion is elsewhere at all in this ratio,— which there is, alas, too much reason for believing to be the case,—it is, most truly, a sad commentary upon the present rendering of Christianity into the character and lives of its professors.

From the facts now submitted, what is the inevitable conclusion? Is it not obviously this? *The piety of the present day has widely degenerated from the divine standard.* Can these facts be accounted for on any other supposition? Look at them in their connection. Christian men, of all denominations and all countries, are deeply impressed with the painful conviction that this is the case. On every hand it is reluctantly, but openly, acknowledged. The totally inadequate supply of Christian ministers confirms the correctness of this general impression; as does also the trifling amount of property consecrated to the dissemination of the gospel in heathen lands. An amount, let it be remembered, not only exceedingly small compared with what might be realized, (and without the sacrifice of any necessary, or even comfort of life,) but gathered at a time when the knowledge of the actual condition of unevangelized nations is generally spread among the churches, thereby rendering inexcusable their inactivity, and gathered, too, not without great labor and expense. And at the same time, the conversion of men in Christian lands progresses but slowly, the "broad way being still the thronged way." Is there any method of accounting for these strange phenomena, we again ask, but that herein assumed? If even a close approximation to the piety of *New Testament* times, in kind and degree, obtained among the churches, how different the moral aspect of the world!

But it may be replied, Are not the churches careful to maintain a sound faith and a wholesome discipline? And are they not discovering a commendable degree of liberality in many of the benevolent enterprises of the day? Are not colleges and seminaries being endowed, and houses of worship built for feeble congregations? And in the social arrangements, and external accommodations of the churches, is there not much to approve and admire?

This is cheerfully and thankfully conceded. Considerations like these essentially relieve the picture of some of its darker aspects. For these, and many other indications of good, let us thank God and take courage. They give promise of a brighter day yet to come. They animate the hope that the cloud shall be lifted from off the church, that her light *shall* come, and the glory of the Lord *shall* arise upon her. Yes; notwithstanding all the imperfections that now adhere to her, the bride of Christ shall yet "look forth as the morning, fair as the moon, clear as the sun, and terrible as an army with banners."

But while it becomes us to entertain a hopeful view of the future, and recognize with gratitude all that which is praiseworthy in the present, it should not be forgotten that man is liable to be deceived from the outward appearance, while "the Lord looketh on the heart." An individual may appear to be in good health, while some deadly disease is preying upon the system. A church may have a name to live, may have a reputation for being alive, while it is, truly, dead. "Thou hast a name that thou livest, and art dead," said Christ, through his servant, to the church in Sardis.

The body of an individual may be in an unsound condition when he himself is not aware of it. And so an individual Christian, or a church, may fall into an *unconscious* decline. Said the prophet of old concerning the kingdom of Israel, "Strangers hath devoured his strength, and he knoweth it not; yea, gray hairs are here and there upon him, yet he knoweth it not." The church in Laodicea was ready to say, "I am rich and increased with goods, and have need of nothing;" but, in fact, it was "wretched, and miserable, and poor, and blind, and naked."

"How many individuals and churches," says one, "are not only flattering themselves that they are in a flourishing condition, but imposing upon others with the same delusion. The place of worship may be commodious, elegant, and free from debt,—the minister popular, and approved by his flock,—the congregation large, respectable, and influential,—the communicants numerous and harmonious,—the finances good, and even prosperous,—the collections for public institutions liberal and regular; in short, there may be every mark of external prosperity, till the church flatters itself, and is flattered by others, into the idea of its being in a high state of spiritual health. It has 'a name to live.' But now examine its internal state,—inquire into its condition as viewed by God,—inspect the private conduct of its members, and ask for the accession of such as shall be saved;

and what a different aspect of things is seen then. How low is the spirit of devotion, as evinced by the neglect of the meetings for *social* prayers; by the omissions in many households of *family* prayer, and by the heartless and irregular manner in which it is maintained in others; and by the giving up, in numerous cases, of *private* prayer. * * * * * *

"Let a stranger, of devotional taste, and spiritual affection, and tenderness of conscience, enter into the families and frequent the parties of such a congregation, and what a destitution would he find of the vitality of religion! Under the deceptive appearance of a large and flourishing assembly, an eloquent preacher, and an air of general respectability and satisfaction on a Sabbath day in the sanctuary, what a deadness of heart would he find; what a prevailing worldliness!"

The most distressing features in this description are its obvious truthfulness, and its breadth of application. The *material* condition of the churches of our country was never as good as at this very day. In some of the elements of influence, intelligence, and property, there has been, of late, a rapid and steady increase.

But the divine injunction, "let him that standeth take heed lest he fall," is as applicable to churches as to individuals. Prosperity is always accompanied with danger. A church is just as liable to be injured by riches as an individual; for what is a church but an aggregation of individuals? If a man come into possession of wealth, we are accustomed to regard it as highly probable that he may become indolent and inactive, perhaps self-conceited and regardless of those in humbler circumstances than himself. But is not the fact too generally lost sight of, that competence is the parent of inactivity and pride, as well in churches as individuals? The prophet Jeremiah says of Moab, he "hath been at ease from his youth, and he hath settled on his lees." Is not the figure applicable to many religious societies, especially those that are possessed of numbers and wealth? Else how can we account for the remarkable fact that more conversions are reported in connection with the smaller than the larger churches? In the one case, the force of circumstances induces untiring activity, which is not only the result, but often the cause of spiritual health. In the other, there being no *ever-present stimulus* urging to continuous personal effort, a living, working faith declined, and the body, though outwardly prosperous, is alarmingly destitute of vitality and power. It is much less difficult to maintain an outward than an inward religion; much less congenial to the partially sanctified heart, to serve God *in person*, than by *proxy*. It requires much less vigilance to maintain a sound *creed* than a sound *heart*. And precisely in this direction lies our chief danger. We are liable to mistake the means for the end; the material for the spiritual.

Benevolent organizations, "Church Order," "Church Architecture," "Church Extension," — all have their importance. They are, however, but the scaffolding of the spiritual temple. Or, to change the figure, they are but the machinery in accomplishing the great work of Christian edification, and the conversion of souls. We may perfect the machinery as much as we will, may improve our Sunday school, educational and missionary organizations, — build commodious and tasteful sanctuaries for ourselves and for others, — may remove errors and imperfections from our articles of faith, and church-discipline; and yet, behind this complete organism, there must be the mighty motive power of *a hidden interior life*, or all is fruitless and vain. These are not the chief good; they are simply the *means to an end.* All this is but *preparatory* work. Something yet lies beyond this, to gain which should be the grand ultimate aim; even growth in grace, and the leading of souls to Christ.

The machinery should be perfect *to do execution;* not that it may be exhibited and admired. The sanctuary should be properly constructed that the Shekinah may rest there, and the divine power and glory be there displayed; not simply to gratify taste, and answer instead of a broken heart and a contrite spirit on the part of the worshipper. Let care be taken as to the material building, but let more concern be felt that the temple within be of "lively stones," built for God. Let Christian men earn money for Christ. Let the rich neither give "the widow's mite," nor suffer their noblest offerings to excuse them from the cultivation of personal religion, and direct efforts to save the perishing around them. Let a sound faith, and a consistent life, and outward benevolence, be but the substantial evidence of a *deep-seated, vigorous piety within.* Let *these* things obtain, and all will be well. Happy were we *did* they obtain! Most happy if there were no real occasion for admonitions like these! But the times imperatively call for such admonitions, since many are being deceived by the illusive covering of an external prosperity; and do not imagine that these outward indications, on the part of churches and individuals, may often be but "as the flowers which bloom in a shallow and sandy soil."

We are compelled to adhere, therefore, to the painful conclusion already stated, that the prevailing piety of the present day is seriously defective; that a worldly spirit has taken possession, to a great extent, of the Christian church, and driven out the sincere, Christlike spirit, that should characterize the saints of the Most High. And until there is a return of that spirit, it is in vain that we expect the world's conversion. That blessed work will not reach its consummation for many thousands of years yet to come, at the present rate of progress of genuine Christianity.

There must be a vast augmentation of moral power in the sacramental host of the Lord. The churches must become vastly more *aggressive* in their operations, — vastly more intent upon executing the sublime commission of the ascended Redeemer.

Indeed the *whole style* of Christian character must be greatly modified, and vitalized, before Zion shall have put on her strength, and having power in herself, shall have power upon the world.

The question as to *what are* the particular defects which most weaken her strength, opens a subject to be hereafter carefully considered.

CHAPTER II.

FIRST GRAND DEFECT OF THE PREVAILING PIETY OF THE TIMES — A WANT OF SIMPLICITY OF PURPOSE.

The "Single Eye." — The True Aim. — "Why am I here?" — *A priori* Argument. — Scripture View. — Why converted. — Christ a Model of Simplicity of Purpose. — Imitated by Early Disciples. — Existing want of Unity of Object. — Vocation not comprehended. — Rage for Money. — Why is Wealth sought? — Divorce of Religion and Business. — Sacrifice to Self. — Perils of Active Pursuits. — Piety and Worldly Care not antagonistic. — Examples. — "My Business Trade." — Varied Services, one End. — Gem from Flavel. — Guilt of living for Unworthy Objects. — Return of Ancient Times. — Christ's Life reproduced. — Glorious Results. — Call for Reform. — Duty of Parents. — Duty of Ministers. — Appeal.

A SINGLE stroke of the Apostolic pen had laid bare a great principle in the religious system: "He that giveth, let him do it *with simplicity*." Let him bestow it without partiality, or vain ostentation; "without seeking the applause of men, or any other sinister end." Let him do it solely to accomplish the one proper object.

The writer who communicated this divine injunction, rejoiced in the testimony of his conscience, "that *in simplicity* and godly sincerity" he had had his conversation among the brethren. He had not been among them to accomplish many, and selfish purposes, but to gain one single end. His affections and energies were not divided between "God and Mammon," but, in keeping with the spirit of our Saviour's instructions, the "eye" was "single," and "the whole body full of light." Not two or more objects, and in a dim, confused light, were present before him, as before a disordered or imperfect eye, but one, clearly discerned object, at which he steadfastly aimed. And this was the secret of the Apostle's success. It is the key to all success; for, by a known law of the mind, its full energies are never put forth unless the object be single.

But what is the *true aim* of life? What one end should man desire to accomplish? It is obvious that God must have had some one great object in view, in the creation of man. He has made nothing in vain. Each little grain of dust, each rock, each rill, each river, each spire of grass, each tree; each living thing, from the mite to the mammoth, the man to the angel, was designed to answer some end, to fill some niche in the great temple of creation.

And yet how few comprehend the design of their creation! "It is to be lamented," said Sir Thomas Smith, in connection with his dying request, "that men know not to what end they were born into the world, until they are ready to go out of it." How few even interrogate themselves as to the end for which they were made! "Why am I here?" "For what was I created?" "Why am I kept in existence?" are questions which most men never seriously consider. They find themselves in the world, and yielding to the force of circumstances, and casting the reins upon the neck of their propensities, they saunter or toil; eat, drink, sleep, and die; having no more lived for any one definite purpose than the bearded goat that browses the mountain shrub, or the gay butterfly that sucks honey from the summer flower.

How strange! As if an ocean steamer, without pilot or rudder, but driven by her giant enginery, were ploughing the deep, and thundering on her way, but bearing no special cargo, and bound to no particular port! As if an angel were coursing hither and thither through the heavens, not knowing the object of his devious flight!

If any other consideration were necessary to render obvious the importance of calling attention to the true aim of life, it were furnished in the fact that so many who do live for some one purpose, have adopted an end entirely unworthy of human existence. Now, in determining the question, What *is* the proper object of man's pursuit? something may be learned from an examination of his character and endowments.

This *à priori* argument runs thus: If, in your travels, you were to fall upon a piece of mechanism, in some respects, at first sight, resembling a watch, and, upon closer examination, found that a slender bar of steel was balanced upon a pivot, which, if undisturbed, always pointed in a given direction, you would not hesitate to pronounce the object of this little instrument to be the indicating of the points of the compass.

From the form and build of a car, a balloon, a boat, you determine as to whether it was designed for a land-carriage, or for the air, or the water. By the same means you are satisfied that the bird is made to chirp, and sing, and fly in the air; and the camel, with his capacious stomach, his thick, tough, elastic foot, and Atlas back, to bear heavy burdens over the broad, burning deserts.

Pursuing the same process of investigation, you place a human being before you, and inquire for what he is designed. You discover that he possesses certain qualities in common with other creatures around him. He has a physical organism, and the principle of animal life. If this were all, it were plain that in hewing wood, and drawing water, and digging the ground, — in caring for himself, and living as lives the brute, regardless of all other than material objects, he were leading a life not unworthy of his being. But these ingredients alone do *not constitute* man. Added to these, you discover another most remarkable element. It is the intelligent principle, the faculty of reason and reflection; the godlike *mind*, the capacious *soul*. This intelligent principle you find to be capable of vast reach and towering strength. There is no limit to its expansion, and it takes no cognizance of time or space in its bold excursions, now into heaven, now into hell, and now to the uttermost parts of the earth. It calls up and ponders on the past, and explores and anticipates the future. It is wise in contriving, far-reaching in execution, and, added to all, is susceptible of the keenest anguish, and the most refined and exquisite enjoyment.

The presence of this most wonderful faculty, forbids the belief that man was designed to pursue no higher purpose, and fill no higher position than that of the unintelligent creation around him. If you were to find the bird of paradise, or the proud eagle, choosing for its abode the foul quagmire, and revelling with the loathsome reptiles that infest it, you would not hesitate to declare that it had suffered a most humiliating degradation. "Most certainly," you would exclaim, "this creature of lovely plumage, or lofty flight, was not made for *such* a life!" If an angel were permitted to assume a mortal body, and should join the multitude of men who delve in the earth to heap up its treasures, and, like them, should live only to gain material wealth, who would not be astonished at his awful depravity, and wonder that such endowments were prostituted to so unworthy an end? On the same principle we cannot err in being persuaded that to eat, and drink, and sleep, and sport away life; or to wear it out in seeking honor, or wealth, or any earthly good, is *not* the end for which man was placed in the world. His lofty endowments find no adequate employment in such pursuits. There is no proper breadth and scope for their action. His giant mind was not made for play. His capacious soul was not intended to be chained down to a clod. No! the eagle was made to soar, — the angel for an angel's service, — and man for *some* exalted, some noble purpose.

But the question as to *what is* that noble purpose for which man is to live, is satisfactorily answered in the Holy Scriptures. It is to glorify God, — to live and labor that God may be honored and loved by his intelligent creatures. Sin has entered into the world; the heart of man is alienated from God; and it is the duty of each to bring back his brother, if he may, to a condition of loyalty and cheerful obedience. The present is a remedial state. God is calling sinners to himself, — he is merciful to their infirmities and sins; and he enjoins it upon us to coöperate with him in his work of mercy. Hence says the apostle, " We then as *workers together with him*, beseech you also that you receive not the grace of God in vain." The divine command comes to each, " Whatsoever ye do, do all to the glory of God." As if it were said, this is the *one simple object* which you are to ever have in view. Indeed, for this object, the glory of God, all things were created. No part of creation, as will be seen in the eternal world, answered its highest end, until it became subservient to this grand design. It will there be seen that "wealth attained its true destination only when it fell into the treasury of Christ; that speech realized its true design only when it became 'a means of grace,' that all the relationships of life, and all the mutual influences with which those relationships invest us," found their proper end only when they harmonized with the divine plan, whose single end is the promotion of the divine glory.

Nor are we left in ignorance as to the *method* of glorifying God. " Herein is my Father glorified, that ye *bear much fruit;*" the fruits of personal obedience and active service. Again, it is written, " put on bowels of mercy;" "put on charity;" "do good to all men;" "ready to distribute, willing to communicate;" "charge them that they do good, that they be rich in good works."

When God bestows his converting grace, it is not only that the individual may be saved, but also that he may promote the salvation of others, to an extent not attained in an unconverted state. Each renewed man is to consider himself as a special messenger of mercy; to do instrumentally what Christ did efficaciously. Said our Saviour, "As thou hast sent me into the world, even so have I also sent them into the world;" or, as Dr. Campbell has it, "As thou hast made me thy apostle to the world, I have made them my apostles to the world." The author of the "*Family Expositor*," gives it thus: "As thou hast sent me into the world to be the messenger of this grace, I also have sent them into the world *on the same errand*, to publish and proclaim what they have learned of me." As though Christ had said to each one of his followers, "I came for one specific purpose, to seek and save that which is lost. Consider yourself as called and dedicated to the same office." Thus are copies of Christ's character, so to speak, multiplied in the lives of his disciples; every renewed soul looking upon himself as the representative of Christ in the world, and bound to go forth beseeching men, in his stead, to be reconciled to God. And Christ himself stands forth to all time, as the finest model, the grandest illustration of this devotedness to life's *one work*. In vain the devil pictures to his mind the kingdoms of the world, and all the glory of them, to be had for one act of deference to his impious authority. In vain the Jews desire to make him a king. In vain the contradiction of sinners. In vain the opposition of wicked men and lying spirits. In vain cold mountains and the midnight air, and even the very calls of nature. He cannot, he will not be turned aside. Still, still are his energies absorbed in *one thing*, still, still is he *going about doing good,* — his whole life the exponent of the sublime sentiment, "*My meat is to do the will of him that sent me, and to finish his work!*"

In imitation of Christ, the *early disciples* were "a peculiar people," because of this singleness of aim. To do good, to make known the great salvation, to lead their fellow men to a knowledge of the truth, was their ruling passion. That they might gain *this* end, they took joyfully the spoiling of their goods, counting not even their lives dear unto them. With this as an ultimate object, they worked with their hands; to gain it, they labored, and thought, and prayed. Like their brethren of the martyr age, their motto, in effect, was, "Nothing for self, every thing for God." Indeed, they looked upon themselves as called into Christ's kingdom with the special design that they might witness for him. This was their *calling*, their *business;* and hence, as they went they preached, and in all places, and all times, sought to win souls to Christ.

Of this simplicity of purpose how bright an example have we in the apostle to the Gentiles, — brighter than that of thousands of others of his time, only because it found a fuller development, and more perfect delineation. It has been well said of him, that there was a time when, in common with the world, he regarded life as superlatively valuable; but he now looked upon it as comparatively insignificant, for he had found an object of unspeakably greater importance. Others might copy the example of their fellow men, but he had risen to the high and holy ambition of copying the example of incarnate perfection, of God manifest in the flesh. Others might waste their precious time in ease, and sloth, and worldly indulgence; but he aspired to enter into the counsels of heaven, to become a coworker with God, and instrumentally to mingle in the operations of almighty love in renewing and blessing a world of apostate but immortal beings. Others might content themselves with the praise of men, with the good opinion of creatures perishing like themselves; but he aspired to the distinction of pleasing God,—of being received and welcomed into the presence of the Supreme, with the sentence, "Well done, good and faithful servant." Others might be satisfied with their own personal salvation; but feeling that he had a Saviour for the world, he panted to go everywhere claiming that world for Christ,—panted to present every man "perfect in Christ Jesus,"—"travailed in birth" for the regeneration of the race."* There was in him an *unity of object.* If he pleased all men, and became "all things to all men," it was that "by any means" he "*might save some.*" If he provoked his brethren to emulation, it was, still, that he "*might save some of them;*" and having this one object before him, he moved onward "with a momentum which the nature of mind forbade to be more, and the principles that actuated him forbade to be less."

The want of this unity of object constitutes a prevailing defect in the Christians of the present day. In this respect they are not followers of the apostles and primitive disciples, as they followed

* Dr. Harris, in "The Great Commission."

Christ. Indeed, the majority of professing Christians seem to entertain no just conception of God's design in introducing them into his kingdom. In their view, they are permitted the privileges of the church, principally if not solely, that they may be *happy* there; that they may "*enjoy* themselves;" rather than that, by a combination of strength, their *usefulness* may be enhanced. The church is rather a nursery, in their view, than a workshop; a place where the pious may quietly regale themselves, in the warm sunshine of the Saviour's love, and the soft breezes of the gracious Spirit, rather than where they may successfully toil and do service for the Master.

The benefit of religion, with them, is, that it imparts a hope of heaven. That which gives them most anxiety, is the question as to whether it is a "good hope;" if satisfied of this, there is little else about which they need concern themselves. They do not comprehend the vocation of the church as a *testifying*, *proselyting* body. They do not sympathize with Christ in the travail of his soul. On that point where God feels the strongest,—the welfare of dying men,—they have little or no feeling. There are no rivers of water running down their eyes, because the people keep not God's law,—no weeping over Jerusalem sinners,—no continual heaviness and sorrow of heart because of the guilt and woe of a sin-stricken world. In a word, they have *no adequate idea* of the one great work to which every child of God is called, and consequently no becoming sympathy in that work. But even where right views are entertained, the pressure of other than the calls of religion oftentimes diverts the energies from the proper object. The energies of some are absorbed in pleasures; or expended in the acquisition of honor; while, in most cases, they are turned toward the accumulation of wealth.

The rage for money, certainly in this country, is a most remarkable feature of the times. "Money answereth all things," it is said; and all things are made to bend to its acquisition. What an English writer has said of his country, is most surely true of ours: "Could we ascertain the entire amount of national excitement and emotion experienced in the course of a year, and could we then distribute it into classes, assigning each respectively to its own exciting cause, who can for a moment doubt that the amount of excitement arising from the influence and operation of money, direct and indirect, would not only exceed that of either of the others, separately considered, but would go near to surpass them altogether?" Go, traverse the streets of our great commercial emporium, and see how the pulse of the community throbs with this tremendous excitement.

As a picture of things twelve months ago, the following, from a resident editor, is not overdrawn: "More lands, more houses, more merchandise, more banks, more railways, more stocks, more and better securities, in one word, more *wealth*. Nobody has any thought of resting satisfied; nobody has business enough, or possessions enough; the city is not yet built, nor is it likely soon to be; every thing is just in its beginning; ship-building and ocean navigation are new arts yet to be developed in their relations to commercial enterprise and wealth; real estate has a chronic fever not likely soon to abate; stocks have an 'upward tendency;' trade is just beginning to be 'lively;' the whole available materials and labor of the world would not suffice to build the railroads projected or contracted for the next twenty years; the machinery of wealth is only put in motion, its results are to be realized; no one yet calls himself rich, but every one means to be rich." *

Now is it selfishness, or benevolence, that begets this universal passion for gain? For, it should be observed, that the desire to possess property is not *in itself* sinful; to seek it may be a virtue, not a vice; to possess it may be a blessing, not a curse. It is not *necessarily* they that have riches that find it hard to enter heaven, but they that *love* riches. It is not money that is "the root of all evil," but the *love* of money.

There is a temple in one of the cities of Europe through which is the very passage to the market-place; and those who pass there, often rest their burdens to turn aside and kneel at the altar of prayer So, as one has said, the temple of Mammon should be the temple of God. The gates of trade should be as the entrance to the sanctuary of conscience. The presence of God is in the counting-room and warehouse of the busy mart, and *ought* to make it "holy ground."

But *do* men, generally, *Christian* men, seek after wealth, and possess it, as in the sight of God, and solely for his glory? If there be this benevolent and not a selfish design in efforts at accumulation, if they

---

* "Independent," March, 1854.

spring from right motives, then are they deserving of commendation, and not reproof; unless, indeed, they are suffered to run to excess. But it is obvious to every discerning mind that this is not the case with the mass of Christian professors. There are some noble exceptions, but it is to be feared that the vast majority regard the end of business as the sustenance of life, or the relief from toil and drudgery for some imaginary enjoyment. Or, which is much the same thing, they regard wealth as an end, instead of a *means to* an end. It was said of a liberal Christian of large ability, subsequent to his death, "he was a man who knew the odds between the means of living, and the ends of life. He knew the true use of riches. They served as the material basis for great, manly excellence. His ton of gold was a power to feed and clothe, to house, and warm, and comfort needy men; a power to educate the mind, to cheer the affections, to bless the soul." Not so of most men. They seek a competence, not that they may glorify God, but glorify themselves, — not that they may use it for the good of the needy, but squander it upon their own lusts, — not that they may make to themselves, with their "mammon of unrighteousness," friends who shall greet them in heaven, and receive them "into everlasting habitations," but that they may live in ease, and make for themselves friends and a great name on earth; or, perhaps, leave a splendid fortune to an idol child, like him of whom one of our own poets hath sung,

> "He had sold his life to gather gain,
> And build a mansion for his only son,
> That crowds might envy. To his wearied heart,

> Amid its slavery, oft he said, 'Plod on,
> '*T is for my son;*'" —

forgetting that that very fortune might prove the curse of the pampered boy, or that, in mercy, God might take him away from the evil to come, leaving one more illustration of the Scripture, "He heapeth up riches, and knoweth not who shall gather them."

Reference is not here had, exclusively, to those who are guilty of downright "covetousness, which is idolatry," a sin of far more frequent occurrence than is generally supposed, as the revelations of the judgment will undoubtedly prove, — nor yet to the poor, miserable creature, well called *miser*,* whose life has been described as "one long sigh for wealth;" who would "coin his lifeblood into gold," and "sell his soul for gain;" who

> "Throws up his interest in both worlds;
> First starved in this, then damned in that to come;"

but principally to men of reputed, and, perhaps, of actual piety.

Is it not a lamentable fact, that with many men of fair character in the Christian church, business is divorced from religion? Do they not pursue it as something *distinct from serving God?* Times and places are sacred; but not the whole of life. *Portions* of time they give to God; but they do not carry their religion into their business. The pew is consecrated to God, but not the counting-room. The hours of the Sabbath they keep holy; but "Holiness to the Lord" is not written upon the *days of the*

---

* Latin *miser*, miserable

week. During the former they *worship God;* during the latter they serve *themselves.* Are not these things so? Are not Christian men too generally actuated in getting money by the *sordid love of gain?* Do they not seek property, not mainly as an instrument of doing good to themselves and others, and by this means promoting the glory of God, but rather out of unworthy and selfish considerations? Is not *industry,* oftentimes, simply another and more respectable name for *worldliness?* Is not the plea, "I must prosecute the business thrown upon my hands, and save the money I have gained," oftentimes, rather an apology for covetousness than the dictate of a sense of duty toward God? And is not the excuse, "I must provide for my family," oftentimes simply an opiate for the conscience, when bowing down and sacrificing to SELF? It cannot be denied. The evidences are too palpable to admit of denial. And it is for this sole reason that active business habits are so destructive to vigorous piety. Business is too often a perfect thraldom, where all the energies are exhausted in the drudgery of mammon, and where the religious affections are wellnigh stifled and destroyed.

It is universally admitted that it is now almost at the peril of his piety that a Christian young man embarks in business, especially if of a commercial or professional character. The experiment is little less hazardous than the shipping of tropical plants to the north pole, or putting one's self into communication with a torpedo. There is a fearful probability that his spiritual energies will be benumbed and stupefied; that he will lose that tender conscience, and that heavenly-mindedness, and sweet simplicity, and hearty sympathy with the cause of the Redeemer, that characterize the young disciple of Christ. And why? Because business is too generally prosecuted from low and selfish motives, and according to other than Christian principles. There is no real antagonism between business and piety. If so, why has God commanded us to be "diligent in business," and at the same time to "grow in grace?" Are not the two things compatible the one with the other? May we not be "*diligent in business, fervent in spirit, serving the Lord?*" This is but an epitome of the lives of *some* business men; which proves that it might be of others. President Edwards tells us of an humble Christian who used to exclaim, "Oh, how good it is to work all day for God, and at night to lie down under his smiles!" And in connection with the narration, he remarks, that "high experiences and religious affections in this person were not attended with any dispositions at all to neglect the necessary business of a secular calling; but worldly business was attended to with great alacrity *as a part of the service of God;* the person declaring that, *being done thus*, it was found to be *as good as prayer*." In this case, active business was found directly conducive to the vigor of the inner life with Christ. Illustrations on the same point are furnished in the lives of Harlan Page, and John Thornton, and Matthew Hale, and William Wilberforce, and Nathaniel R. Cobb, and Garrat Noel Bleecker, — all of whom, amid pressing duties and responsibilities of a worldly nature, were eminent for piety and good works. Normand Smith, who lived and died at Hartford, Connecticut, — died exclaiming, "*Home, home, — I see the New Jerusalem, — They praise Him — they praise Him!*" — was another bright example of a *business Christian.** Involved in an extensive business, he was, at one time, led to inquire, whether it was not his duty to relinquish it, at least in part, that he might have time to do more good. Seeking the advice of his pastor,† he was told that "the Lord, in prospering him, had indicated how he was to glorify him in the world. It was urged that the channels of wealth were open, and their streams flowing in upon him, and that it would be wrong to obstruct them, — that pursuing his business out of a sense of duty, that he might do good, and so honor God, he would increase in holiness and usefulness." It appears that shortly after this conversation he made the following entry in his journal: "The Lord has made the path of duty plain before me; for a year I have been in much doubt as to the duty of continuing my present business. My mind has become settled. I have determined to continue it, and I trust it is not in order to grow rich. I dare not be rich. I would not be rich. 'They that would be rich fall into temptation,' etc. I believe the Lord has led me, and inclined me to pursue my business, not to increase in riches, but that I may have to give to him that needeth. It is therefore my purpose to engage in

* The incidents of his life here given, are gathered from his biography, written by Rev. Joel Hawes, D. D., and published by the American Tract Society.

† The biographer.

my business that I may serve God in it, and with the expectation of getting to give." From that time it became his rule to use for benevolent purposes all the means which he could take from his business, and prosecute it advantageously; and the Lord blessed him richly, and made him, by his consistent piety and active usefulness, a rich blessing to others. His whole life, and his triumphant death, were a beautiful commentary upon the fact that business, *rightly pursued*, instead of being hostile to active piety and extensive usefulness, is of a nature precisely the opposite.

His biographer tells us that he never grew in grace more rapidly, or shone brighter as a Christian than during the last six or seven years of his life, when he had the greatest amount of business on his hands. From the time when he devoted all to God, and resolved to pursue his business as a part of his religion, he found no tendency in his worldly engagements to chill his piety or enchain his affections to the earth. His business became to him a *means of grace*, and helped him forward in the divine life, just as truly as reading the Scriptures and prayer.

Let the motives and principles of this devoted Christian be generally adopted, and the complaint would cease to be made, that the toils and cares of life choke the word of grace, and cause it to become unfruitful.

Thus ordered, the office or the shop becomes a very Bethel. The disciple must exemplify the doctrines and spirit of his Lord on the farm, or the exchange, as in the closet; and flocks and herds, and money and merchandise, do but remind him of his stewardship, and quicken the sense of his obligations to God and a dying world.

Thus ordered, "one's whole life, its pauses and retirements, its Sabbaths and its solemn assemblies, will be one long act of consecration. The psalm of a grateful and regenerate heart will, with its habitual, unremitting flow, fill up all the interstices of his visits to the closet and the sanctuary. The life of godliness will be devotional even on common days and in familiar scenes. It will thus bring down beams and airs of heaven, into earth's darkest and lowliest nooks. Its calendar will have its whole year hallowed; while it keeps still its days of special sanctity, the thrice hallowed. It will be WORSHIP AT WORK, kneading the leaven of Christian principle into the entire mass of its personal activity and social influence."* "No Christian has a right to regard his business as separate from the honor of his Maker, and the good of his fellow men. *His* interests should be identified with the interests of the church and the glory of his Saviour; and whenever his time or personal influence is demanded to promote a good work, he should be ready to meet the demand,— considering only whether in this way he can best serve God and his generation. This is the true principle of action, and it ought to be adopted by every Christian man of business. No Christian man has a right to make his business paramount to the demands of Christian duty, or so to burden himself with secular cares, as to find no time to do good. Indeed, the man who is most deeply engaged in

---

* Worship at Work. American Tract Society.

business, if *he feels right*, is usually the man who is most ready unto every good work. For in all his aims and intercourse with this world, he has a simple purpose to glorify God." *

O how imperative the demand for more of this oneness of aim!

"In his case," said a merchant, referring to a minister of the gospel, "in his case the promotion of religion was his chief business; but *my* business is trade, which requires the exercise of different faculties and different rules of life." Here the whole difficulty presents itself. "The promotion of religion was *his business*," "*Mine is trade!*" As if what is the minister's business, is not the business of the private Christian! As if it were some men's vocation to serve Christ, and that of some to serve themselves! As if "trade" were incompatible with serving the Lord, and must be prosecuted according to "different rules!"

Alas, these pernicious maxims of the times, to what an alarming extent do they prevail in the church of Christ!

How simple, and yet explicit the divine injunction, "Ye are not your own; for ye are bought with a price: therefore, *glorify God in your body and in your spirit, which are God's.*" Here every thing is plain. The disciples of Christ follow, of necessity, different pursuits; but, of right, they alike follow them for *one end.* The occupation is different, — the *object* the same. "Bought with a price," they are to serve, and thus glorify God. Some are called to serve at

* See Life of N. Smith, p. 61.

the counter, some at the anvil, some at the loom, some at the carpenter's bench, some at the bench of justice, — some by ploughing the deep waters, some by ploughing the warm soil, — some by preaching, some by teaching, — some with the hand, some with the mouth, some with the brain; but all, in every department of activity, are under the most sacred obligations to make the promotion of religion, either directly or indirectly, their chief business, their ONE GRAND AIM!

Any other view than this, of Christian obligation, is every way inadequate and unworthy. Redeemed for a noble, godlike purpose, as is the believer, how low, how grovelling the love of pelf, and the pursuit of it for mere selfish ends! In the words of an old gem from Flavel,

"Judge in thyself, O Christian! Is it meet
To set thy heart on what beasts set their feet?
'T is no hyperbole, if you are told
You dig your dross with mattocks made of gold.
Affections are too costly to bestow
Upon the fair-faced nothings here below;
The eagle *scorns* to fall down from on high,
The proverb saith, to catch the silly fly;
And can a *Christian* leave the face of God,
To embrace the earth, or doat upon a clod?"

But this turning aside from the one work of seeking the welfare of dying men, has in it, also, the element of *guilt*, of exceeding wickedness in the sight of God. Suppose that during the prevalence of the awful famine that visited unfortunate Ireland, a few years since, twenty men had been intrusted with a cargo of grain which had been purchased with the funds of the benevolent, and was put into their charge to be shipped to the famine-stricken people, and distributed for their relief.

And suppose that, on their way, the men should have stopped at some intervening port, and becoming acquainted with extraordinary commercial advantages there presenting themselves, and ceasing to feel any special interest in the mission of mercy on which they had been sent, or obligations to those that sent them, they had abandoned the object contemplated, and actually consumed the property consigned to their care, or traded it away, and with the avails established themselves in some splendid commercial enterprise. What awful guilt! What unfaithfulness to those who had confided in them! What worse than brutal insensibility to the cries and distresses of those who were dying for want of the aid which they were able, and in duty bound to bestow! But is it not infinitely more guilty in men to turn aside from the benevolent mission to which every Christian is appointed, and prostitute their affections and energies and means to the promotion of their own selfish designs, while multitudes perish from their unconcern and neglect! O for the simplicity of ancient times! when men and women, whatever their *mode* of doing good, could say with the Apostle, though in another sense, "*One thing I do*," — when "one all-pervading passion, one all-controlling purpose, bound their various and versatile efforts together, causing the whole to result, like the intricate motions of a complicated machine, in one entire effect." O for the time when each believer in Christ will feel that he is singled out, and appointed by the Master to perform daily service in his vineyard; not necessarily by neglecting the business pursuits and complicated affairs of life, but *for that very purpose* attending to them, — the time when parents shall love and educate their children *for Christ's sake*, — when the tradesman shall eagerly watch opportunities of honest gain, that he may withdraw so much of the wealth of the world from sordid purposes, and consecrate it to the advancement of the cause of the Redeemer, — when the scholar, the lawyer, the farmer, the tradesman, the mechanic, shall attend to the duties of his vocation out of a desire to glorify him who loved us and gave himself for us, — when, in a word, every disciple, not waiting for some *great* opportunities of usefulness, shall seize the *present* opportunities, and do the work that lies in his own sphere of action, remembering that " as the course of Christ led directly to the cross, *his* life is to be a continuation of the same course, from the cross to the sinner whom it concerns; so that the *same object* for which his Lord came into the world and died, he is to live for till he quits the world." Then were the life of Christ reproduced in the life of his followers. Then were Christendom full of active minds and active hands planning and plying their business with the sublime end of saving men from the power and dominion of sin and death. Then were there no need of startling appeals and expensive machinery to bring a few thousands of dollars into the treasury of the Lord, but the rich, by contributing of their abundance, and the poor of their poverty, would more than supply the largest demand. There were then no want of Aarons and Hurs, and Priscillas and

Aquilas, to stay up the hands of God's ministers, and act as "helpers in Christ Jesus," for "the people" would have "a mind to work."

How industrious and how prudent would men then become! How "diligent in business" and economical of their means, that they might have wherewith to feed the hungry, and clothe the naked, and impart to all the knowledge of Jesus! How cheerfully and happily, then, would mothers encounter the little trials, and meet the numerous grave responsibilities incident to the training of their children *for Christ and his cause!* With what a glad heart would fathers toil and swelter in the noonday sun, to provide for their household! Doing it "*as unto God*," and finding it as conducive to piety as is prayer. With what moral grandeur would our shops and counting-houses be then invested, where busy minds and busy hands were occupied in getting gain for the sublime purpose of carrying out the designs of the King of Heaven! And how greatly multiplied would be the number of the strong men, the *efficient workers* in our churches; for, as has been observed, "the grand idea of toiling to rescue the world from sin, never mastered a man's soul without enlarging it, without stimulating all his faculties to unprecedented vigor, unfolding resources not yet imagined to be in him, and producing a concentration and perseverance of action, which cannot fail of realizing great results."

Such would be some of the happy results attendant upon a prevailing simplicity of purpose among God's dear children. And in vain do we look for the highest success of the gospel, until this trait of character obtains to a far greater extent than it now obtains.

In this matter there must be an entire reform. Christian character must assume more of that "moral fitness which springs from disinterested devotedness to the one object of the world's salvation," before it will possess its true beauty and power.

The Redemptorists, a corps of young Romish priests, among all their errors, adopted this excellent rule for their daily life: Before you begin your work, say, "*All for thee, O Lord; O my Jesus, all for thee!*" The significant watchword of the zealous Loyola was, "*Ad majorem Dei Gloriam*"—*for the greater glory of God!* And it was the pious Swinnock of the seventeenth century who said, "I desire that I may never, in a morning, open my shop, or lift up a tool, (as my trade is,) before I have lifted up my heart to God for his blessing upon my endeavors."

O for the prevalence of sentiments like these, among the ranks of Christ's followers! To render them universal, is truly a most worthy object of Christian endeavor.

In this work pious fathers and mothers have an important part to perform. Erroneous views respecting the great end of life are, to a fearful extent, instilled into the minds of children, by well-meaning but misguided parental example and instruction. In the majority of instances, the child is led to the conclusion that to "make money" and "save money" and "lay up money" is verily the chief, if not the sole object which he must steadily keep in view. Toward that object every energy is to be directed.

He has heard his father's creed, that is made up of various time-honored and accredited maxims touching "*the way to get rich;*" and to "get rich" is his highest aim.

"As the twig is bent, the tree 's inclined."

They that rock the cradle rule the world. The child is father to the man; and when he is converted to Christ it is next to impossible to change the drift and current of his mind, and turn it in a benevolent direction. Christian parents must eschew these pernicious maxims, and in their stead teach their sons and daughters the precepts of "pure religion." They must inculcate the lessons of industry and economy, that their children form not indolent or prodigal habits, but, at the same time, teach them the *true use* of riches; that they should seek property, not to love it, and hoard it up; but to scatter it abroad as a means of doing good. In fine, they must lead them to understand by careful instruction, and by their personal example, that the end of life is *not to please themselves*, but to *glorify God.*

Ministers of the gospel, above all, have a most important work to do in causing this unity of object to become more prevalent. First of all, if they have lost sight of the one great object of their vocation, they should themselves seek for purity of motive and directness of aim. And it is to be feared that in this matter, the ministers as well as the churches come far short of attaining to the inspired standard. It is to be feared that some, at least, within the sacred profession, are influenced by other motives than the simple desire to glorify God in saving souls.

The danger of being actuated by personal considerations, is greater than is generally supposed. It requires much prayer and constant watchfulness, in order to lose sight of one's self, and be kept entirely free from the desire and attempt to please his fellow men rather than God. Alas that *one* called to "watch for souls," should suffer himself to be diverted, in the least degree, from his great work, by a desire to accumulate this world's goods! Alas that *one* should expend his energies in preparing to display his wit; or, by culling flowers and polishing his sentences, to court the approbation of his hearers, and be called a man of learning, and of "a powerful imagination," an "eloquent preacher!" The minister's "eye," above all other men, should "be single." He should labor, and pray, and preach, for *one thing*, even the salvation of men. He is surrounded by dying men, whom he should seek with all his might to snatch from "everlasting burnings." And should these words meet the eye of one who has, to any extent, become indifferent to this great object, to him, especially, is commended what Baxter has said in his "Reformed Pastor:" "Many a time have I known that I had some hearers of higher fancies, that looked for rarities, and were addicted to despise the ministry, if I told them not something more than ordinary; and yet I could not find it in my heart to turn from the necessities of the impenitent, for the humoring of them; nor even to leave speaking to miserable sinners for their salvation, in order to speak so much as should otherwise be done to weak saints, for their confirmation and increase in grace. Methinks as Paul's spirit was 'stirred within him' when he saw the Athenians 'wholly given to idolatry,' so it should cast us into one of his paroxysms, to see so many men in the greatest danger of being everlastingly undone. Methinks that if by faith we did indeed look upon them as within a step of hell, it would more effectually untie our tongues, than Crœsus' danger did his son's. He that will let a sinner go down to hell for want of speaking to him, doth set less by souls than did the Redeemer of souls; and less by his neighbor than common charity will allow him to by his greatest enemy. O, therefore, brethren, whomsoever you neglect, neglect not the most miserable! Whatever you pass over, forget not poor souls that are under the condemnation and curse of the law, and who may look every hour for the infernal execution, if a speedy change do not prevent it. O call after the impenitent, and ply this great work of converting souls, whatever else you leave undone."

But it is not enough that the minister of Christ possess this simplicity of purpose; he must secure its existence, so far as lies in his power, on the part of the people committed to his charge. This is to be effected, mainly, by unfolding the great principles of the gospel, in their application to secular pursuits. The relations of business and religion need to be more fully developed. Men must be taught to bring their worldly avocations within the pale of religion. They must be educated into the belief that laymen and ministers are to live and labor for ONE *and the same object*, though in the matter of *directness* there exists a difference in accomplishing that object. It must be shown to them that secular pursuits may be made sacred,—that any legitimate calling, if pursued in a proper manner, and with right ends, is rendered, in the best sense of the term, a "*sacred* calling,"—and that unless it is rendered such, it is pursued in a manner unworthy of the Christian's high vocation.

At this very point business men imperatively need the help of the pulpit. It is high time that it was extended to them by the more frequent discussion of these great topics. Who, if not ministers, shall help those who are called to grapple with the temptations and trials of active business life, to entertain correct views, elevate their aim, and foster an abiding sense of their obligations to God and their fellow men?

Reader! Have you adopted as yours the *true aim* of life? And is its attainment the object of your most abiding, your strongest desire? Are you "jealous for the Lord God of Hosts?" Are you watching for opportunities of doing good? Is your conversation such as becometh saints? And your speech, is it always "with grace, seasoned with salt?" Are you accustomed to speak a word for Christ when you may? and in your intercourse with impenitent men, to speak kindly and earnestly to them of Jesus and eternity? And in your daily labors, do you toil out of love to Christ, and because it is pleasing to God? Have you, in a word, a simplicity of aim and purpose to serve God? Be exhorted to examine into your motives, and answer these interrogations honestly, as in the sight of God. "The heart of man is deceitful;" and even the true Christian may imagine that he is actuated by purely benevolent motives, when at the same time it is quite the reverse. Do not, therefore, dismiss this subject until you have given to it your most careful and prayerful consideration.

Wicked men and the great enemy of Christ are bringing accusations against God; consider yourself as subpœnaed to witness for the truth: "Ye are my witnesses, saith the Lord." You are as truly called to diffuse the gospel as is the minister to preach it. Indeed, you are yourself to preach it; personally, by the fireside and the way-side, wherever and whenever you find an unconverted sinner; and indirectly by providing for its dissemination by others. God comes to you, my friend, and lays his claim upon your time and your property, upon every power of your body or mind, and every affection of your heart. Acknowledge the claim. It is just. You are his by creation, and you are "redeemed with a price." O what a price! Not "with corruptible things, as silver and gold," but "with the precious blood of Christ, as of a lamb without blemish and without spot." "*The precious blood of Christ!*" If he has given his "*blood*" for you, is it too much that you should give your poor imperfect services, and your paltry silver and gold to him? In giving it to his cause you are giving it to him. He accounts as done for himself whatever you do for one whom he loves. Arise, then, and work for Christ! Go about "*doing good!*" Let the golden cord of love bind together life's threads into *unity of purpose*, and you shall not live in vain. With the beating of every pulse your fellow-mortals are passing to their fearful doom! Another hour, and hundreds of them will have gone! Have you any thing to do for their salvation? Do it quickly, — do it with your might! Nor be less diligent to save from perdition those about you; for it shall be more tolerable for the heathen, in the day of judgment, than for them.

"Christian, view the day
Of Retribution! Think how ye will bear
From your Redeemer's lips the fearful words,
'Thy brother, perishing in his own blood,
Thou saw'st. — Thy brother hungered, was athirst,
Was naked, — and thou saw'st it. He was sick,
Thou didst withhold the healing; was in prison
To vice and ignorance, — nor didst thou send
To set him free.' Oh! ere that hour of doom,
Whence there is no reprieve, brother, awake
From this dark dream!"

CHAPTER III.

SECOND GRAND DEFECT IN THE PIETY OF THE PRESENT DAY,—THE WANT OF A JUST MEASURE OF CONSECRATION TO GOD.

Nature of Consecration.—Is its Spirit, as evinced at the time of Conversion, retained?—Sin of robbing God.—Unsanctified Affections.—Property not consecrated.—Root of the Evil.—Insidious Nature of Covetousness.—God's Hatred of this Sin.—Liability of being contaminated by it.—Results as to the spread of the Gospel.—Early Disciples and Moravians.—Cause of insufficient Supply of Preachers.—Of Inefficiency of Prayer.—Where to apply the Remedy.—Alphabet of the Doctrine of Stewardship not yet learned.—Heart to be wholly consecrated.—Thus escape the Perils of Wealth.—Power within and Impression without.—Holiness not attained without Effort.—Why unsought.—Our Lord required Retirement.—Piety sent back to Home-altar and Closet.—An elevated Standard.—Aids in attaining it.—Knowledge of Scripture Doctrine.—Other means indicated.—Personal Interrogations.—Luther in the Pulpit.—President Edwards.—Tests of Covetousness.

WHEN the people of Collatia were entering into stipulations about their surrender to the authority and protection of Rome, the question was asked, "Do you deliver up yourselves, the Collatine people, your city, your fields, your water, your bounds, your temples, your utensils, all things that are yours, both hnman aud divine, into the hands of the people of Rome?" And, on their replying, "we deliver up all,"—they were received.

The incident affords a beautiful illustration of *a*

becoming consecration to God, on the part of the believer, — a subject now proposed for examination.

The *first* duty of the renewed soul is to gain a distinct view of the design of God in his creation and conversion. The question which he should honestly propose, and intelligently and prayerfully settle. is, "Lord, what wilt thou have me to do?" Guided by the Scriptures of divine truth, he perceives that the one work to which he is called, is the promotion of God's glory in the earth, a subject already considered. As the next step in the path of duty, he is to place himself in a position to accomplish life's great work by consecrating to that end all his powers and possessions.

The claim which God makes upon man, as has been previously stated, covers all his intellectual and physical energies, all his property, and all his affections. The believer is cheerfully to respond to this demand of the Almighty, acknowledging its justness, and saying with that ancient people to their superiors, "I deliver up all."

That this claim, on the part of God, is *just*, is obvious from the simple consideration that we are *his*, not our own: his by creation and by redemption. And that it is thus *comprehensive*, is evident from such Scriptures as the following: "Thou shalt love the Lord thy God, with all thy heart, and with all thy soul, and with all thy mind." * "Glorify God in your body, and in your spirit, which are God's." † "As every man hath received the gift, even so min-

---

* Matt. 22: 37. † 1 Cor. 6: 20.

ister the same one to another, as good stewards of the manifold grace of God." *

The nature of this transaction between God and man, is further discoverable in the character of one's exercises when awakened to a sense of sin, and led to inquire, "what shall I do to be saved?" Recur to your own experience. When sensible of your guilt and danger, — when weary and heavy laden you sought for rest, — did the Saviour speak peace to your troubled soul, until you were ready to yield up all to him? — until you could from the heart exclaim,

> "Lord, I make a full surrender,
> Every power and thought be thine;
> Thine entirely, through eternal ages thine?"

You may have attempted, for a time, to compromise the matter; and virtually said, "Lord, I wish to make this single reservation, — I wish to retain one friend, — to consider as mine a few hundreds of dollars, — or to follow my favorite pursuit, and not forsake *every thing* for thee." But all in vain. You found no peace; the burden was still upon the soul: until, at last, the language of your soul was, "I surrender, Lord; take away this burden of sin, and admit me into thy favor; I keep back nothing, I deliver up *all.* Lord, what wilt thou have me to do?" It was then, and not until then, that you could safely lay hold of the hope set before you in the gospel.

Such is the nature of an adequate Christian con-

---

* 1 Peter, 4: 10.

secration. It will be perceived that it is the precise opposite of that selfishness that reigns in the natural heart. And this abasement of self, and exaltation of God, is the grand characteristic of that *holiness* which the Scriptures enjoin upon the followers of Christ. For, as one has observed, "the very core of all religion is not to live to ourselves, but to God; not to consider ourselves our own, but the property and servants of Jesus Christ; not to feel as though we are set up in the world to work for ourselves, to spend the most of our time in promoting what is termed our innocent gratifications, but to hold our time, powers, influence, and property, as talents intrusted to us to be used for Christ, keeping our eye on his lips, to learn his will, and aiming habitually to please and honor him."

But is that spirit of entire consecration which characterizes the believer as he enters the kingdom of Christ, generally *retained*, or is it, to a great extent, soon lost? The thought of withdrawing from God what we have yielded up to him, is one from which we may well recoil. Is it not, indeed, an awful sin,—that of *robbing God!*—recalling and disowning our solemn vows!—promising to serve and obey our Redeemer *wholly*, and then, when once in a supposed saved state, becoming alienated in heart, and virtually claiming and taking back from him what we had most sacredly surrendered?

But it is too obvious from the worldly, unsanctified state of the mass of God's professed people, that they have thus departed from the vows of their consecration. What an apparent inappropriateness, if applied to Christians of our day, is there in such expressions of the Scriptures as the following: "dead unto sin," — "alive unto God," — "that ye bear much fruit," — "the world is crucified unto me, and I unto the world," — "crucified with Christ," — walking "not after the flesh, but after the Spirit," — "not conformed to this world," but "transformed by the renewing of the mind," — "let us cleanse ourselves from all filthiness of the flesh and spirit, perfecting holiness in the fear of God," — "be ye *holy* for *I* am holy," — "filled with all the fulness of God," — "that your love may abound more and more," being "filled with all the fruits of righteousness," — "perfect in every good work," — "sanctify you wholly," — "your whole spirit and soul and body be preserved blameless unto the coming of our Lord." It would almost seem as if such language were descriptive of some other beings than ourselves; or, that it must be some way modified, before it can be applicable to Christians in this age. Nevertheless, it is the divine standard of consecration, to which believers of all ages are commanded to attain. And that they so generally, and so widely, fail of its attainment, is a fearful omen as regards the final acceptance of many in heaven, who are accepted by the church upon earth. It justifies, perhaps, the strong language of an eminent Christian minister, who says, "I tremble for multitudes all around. Never, no, never were professors more in danger of *self-deception* than in this age. If the standard of true religion be the New Testament, then, no small portion of the members of all our churches cannot be true Christians. . . . . Let any one study the Bible descriptions of holiness, —

the setting forth of sanctification as we find it in our Lord's sermon on the mount, — the sixth, eighth, and twelfth chapters of the Epistle to the Romans, — the thirteenth of the first Epistle to the Corinthians, — the third chapter of the Epistle to the Ephesians and Philippians, — and the address of our Lord to the seven churches in Asia, in the book of Revelation, — and say if our churches will stand this test." *

But if the *affections* of Christians are not wholly consecrated to God, so neither are their *possessions.* It is, indeed, true that there are few who do not *in theory* understand and admit the doctrine that what they possess belongs to God, — that their property, their children, their all, they simply hold as stewards, the command being, "occupy till I come." But *practically* this doctrine is almost universally repudiated. Into but few minds has it entered as an ever abiding, earnest conviction.

The great mass of property in the Christian church is *unconsecrated* property. It is sought and possessed for selfish purposes; it is not dedicated to God, and used with an eye single to his glory. "The root" of "this evil," is the *love* of *money,* an *inordinate* love of money, generally termed *covetousness,* — the easily besetting sin of the world, — the great foe of Christianity, exceedingly sly and artful, exceedingly liable to escape unsuspected and unreproved, even in the bosom of the Church. For, while it is impossible for a profane man or a drunkard to maintain a reputable standing in the church, a covetous man may

* See "Course of Faith," p. 100.

do this, because the sin is *within*, and, perhaps, because the avaricious man is looked upon by his brethren too charitably; and a sin in which it is believed that he is indulging, is not made a matter for admonition and church-discipline.

Now that this is a sin peculiarly displeasing to God, is manifest from its repeated and terrible denunciations in the Scriptures. Once did God visibly mark the murderer, (Gen. 4: 15,) — once did he inflict an awful punishment upon the Sabbath-breaker, (Numb. 15: 36,) — once did he cause the visible penalty to be visited upon the head of the blasphemer, (Lev. 24: 10, 15,) but how many fell beneath his displeasure for the violation of the command, "*Thou shalt not covet!*" Achan saw the Babylonish garment and the golden wedge, and he "coveted them and took them," and for the act was stoned to death. Lot, out of the love of gain entered the wicked city, became involved in grossly sinful acts, and finally was stripped of all his possessions. Judas sold his Lord for gain, and how fearful his end! And Ananias and Sapphira, through covetousness and hypocrisy stained the glory of the primitive church, and were *smitten* down by the wrath of the Almighty. It is a sin which God has classed and made synonymous with the abominations of the heathen world, — *idolatry.* "This ye know that no whoremonger, nor unclean person, nor covetous man who is an idolater, hath any inheritance in the kingdom of Christ and of God." "Mortify, therefore, your members . . . . . inordinate affection, evil concupiscence, and covetousness which is idolatry, for which things' sake the wrath of God cometh on the children of disobedience." "Nor thieves, nor covetous, nor drunkards, nor revilers, nor extortioners, shall inherit the kingdom of God." And it is marked as one of the grand features of the final apostasy: "This know, also, that in the last days perilous times shall come. For men shall be lovers of their own selves, covetous, boasters, proud, blasphemers," etc.

Nor is it surprising that this sin is represented as so exceedingly aggravated; for it is the "*monopoly of guilt;*" it combines and absorbs into itself all other species of wickedness. "Could we only see it embodied, what a monster should we behold! Its eyes have no tears. With more than the fifty hands of the fabled giant, it grasps at every thing around. In its march through the world, it has been accompanied by artifice and fraud, rapine and injustice, cruelty and murder; while behind it have dragged heavily its swarms of victims, — humanity bleeding, and justice in chains, and religion expiring under its heavy burdens, orphans and slaves and oppressed hirelings, — a wailing multitude, reaching to the skirts of the horizon." *

And yet, our extreme liability to become contaminated by this awful sin, is apparent from those very denunciations; from the history of our race; from the depravity of our nature; and from the many warnings against its insidious approach. "*Take heed,*" said our Saviour, "and *beware of covetousness:*" that is, Be on your watch against it; have a singular and special regard to it; as if it were a stealthy foe;

---

* Dr. Harris in Mammon, p. 138.

like the imaginary demon, which was fabled to slyly approach and suck the blood of persons while they were asleep.

Alas, that facts should so abundantly justify the necessity of such warnings! Alas, that with them all, so many should fall beneath its power, and pierce their souls through with many sorrows! What open apostasy has it caused among professed Christians! How many who "did run well" have been "hindered" by the golden bait that fell in their path! There are doubtless many in our churches who are guilty of this sin, and, at the same time utterly unconscious of it. The frosts of autumn and winter creep over the meadow, knit their transparent covering upon the face of the pools, and seal up the running streams, so gradually and noiselessly as to elude all observation. So has this accursed love of money crept upon many a heart, chilled its warm out-gushings, and wellnigh frozen up the very fountains of benevolence; and yet so insidiously has the fearful process advanced, that the individual has perceived it not.

And let it not be supposed that this representation applies to the *rich* alone. It is a common belief that men of wealth, principally, if not exclusively, are exposed to covetousness; and hence the poor, and those of limited means, are more readily drawn into its snare. The former class may be more liable to indulge cupidity than the latter; nevertheless, a man who has, or desires, but a small sum, may set his heart just as firmly upon those few hundreds of dollars, as does the rich man upon his many thousands. Indeed, the circumstance of limited means, and the necessity of industry and economy, very naturally lead to a parsimonious spirit. Beyond question a frequent method of approach on the part of this deceitful sin, is by soliciting the poor man, under this very disguise. "It may yoke him as a captive to its car, though he may appear to be only keeping poverty at bay. He need not plunge into the ocean in order to drown himself, — a very shallow stream will suffice, if he chooses to lie prostrate in it; and the desire of the smallest gain, if his heart be immersed in the pursuit, will as surely 'drown him in perdition,' as if the object of his cupidity were the wealth of a Crœsus."

With these considerations before the mind, who can doubt but that this immoderate love of ourselves and the things wherewith we are intrusted, and, consequently, this robbing of God by not yielding up to him that which is his due, is a most frequent, as well as aggravated sin? And what are its consequences and practical results? Fearful in the extreme.

Hence languishes the cause of missions; lying, like Lazarus at the gate of Opulence, where *Christians* fare sumptuously every day, or, like a crouching mendicant, "wandering among the churches, soliciting with a pauper's importunity the shreds and parings of liberal incomes, and then proclaiming at every corner the name and residence of every donor of a half shekel, lest, forsooth, unless his reluctantly bestowed contribution should be loudly trumpeted, he might cease to care for the will of the Lord Jesus, and lose his interest in the salvation of a world, and the missionary treasury feel no more of the overflowings of his benevolence."

How changed the scene were each believer to arise in the dignity of a child of the Most High, and from the heart exclaim,

> "Here on thy altar, Lord, I lay
> My soul, my life, my *all;*
> To follow where thou lead'st the way,
> To obey thy every call!"

Thus entire was the consecration of the disciples who composed the first gospel church; and who has not been impressed with this perfect conformity, in their lives and manners, with the principles of religion? Read the second chapter of the Acts of the Apostles, and behold what a happy community of sentiment and feeling, and what a generous and unaffected liberality to all the brethren. Neither by the teachings of our Lord, nor of the apostles, was it enjoined upon the members of this infant body to give up their property into a common stock; for it is asked of one, "while it remained was it not thine own, and after it was sold, was it not in thine own power?" but, with an entire voluntariness, those who had possessions, without the least hesitancy parted with them, that the less favored might be supplied. "The multitude of them that believed were of one heart and of one soul, *neither said any of them that ought of the things which he possessed* WAS HIS OWN." As one has observed, "they possessed as not possessing, regarding all but as held in trust for the Lord's service, and always ready for any claims which that service made."* The presence of this

* Kitto in Apostles and Early Church.

spirit, or even an approximation to it, would secure for our mission treasuries, millions where now there are but hundreds or thousands.

The Moravians are few in number, not exceeding twenty thousand, and possessed of but comparatively little wealth, and yet they sustain seventy missionary stations with two hundred missionaries, at an annual expense of $60,000.* If the members of evangelical churches in the United States contributed, severally, in the same proportion, for foreign missionary purposes, more than *eleven millions of dollars* would be received; a sum four times greater than that now received from all the churches of both England and America; and *fourteen* times greater than that contributed by the churches in the United States. O that even *this* measure of the spirit of primitive piety generally obtained! For want of its presence how lingers the world's salvation!

Moreover it is precisely *this* defect in our piety, this want of an adequate Christian consecration, that underlies the whole matter of ministerial destitution. "How many there are in our churches," to adopt the language of an able religious journal, "who are lamenting the paucity of ministers, perhaps that they cannot find one for their own church, — lamenting that so few young men are candidates for the sacred office, — lamenting the want of unreserved and sustained zeal in the ministry, — who, if

---

* It has been recently stated that money is contributed for the support of these missions, by individuals in England, who do not belong to the Moravian church; but to what amount it does not appear.

they would question their own hearts, would find that they would be unwilling themselves to be ministers, or to have their sons or brothers the subjects of such a lot." And well is it added, "here lies the difficulty, — in this half-hearted consecration to Christ. Time was when mothers knelt over their children in the cradle, and prayed that God would make them ministers; — now how many pray that God would make them any thing else! Time was when the churches sought out acceptable gifts, and urged the possessors to a work, which, though hard and responsible, was an honorable distinction; now, alas, the general indisposition to the ministry, renders it a painful thing to ask anybody to enter it. At any rate, not the rich must give their sons to the work; they may be lawyers, physicians, merchants; the poor only must be taken, and the rich that withhold their own sons may compromise with the Saviour of their souls by contributing to the Education Society. God forgive us all! The mischief is a radical one. It is found in our meagre notions of Christian consecration and Christian duty. We may lament as much as we will; we may multiply colleges and theological seminaries to any extent; but until we have a spirit of consecration in our churches, such as shall make us all willing to be ministers, if that were Christ's will, and to have our sons and brothers ministers, whatever our rank or station in life may be, and to account even hardness an acceptable service, we shall still find the harvest plenteous and the laborers few."

And to what other cause than that herein indicated shall be ascribed our inefficiency in prayer and other Christian duties? The Scriptures speak of "praying with all prayer," praying "without ceasing," and of the "fervent, effectual prayer" that "availeth much;" and they record instances not a few of the power of prayer to *move the arm that moves* the world. Occasionally men who are mighty with God are met with in our day. Perhaps they are ministers of the gospel; and as was said of one, when they pray, "it is right into the heart of God," and when they preach, "it is right into the heart of the sinner." But are not such men always and eminently the temples of the Holy Ghost, consecrated to the Master's service, and surrounded by the atmosphere of the throne? And can we look for a large increase of their number, until the Spirit be poured out upon us from on high; regenerating, as it were, our regeneration, converting our conversion, and lifting us into a higher and holier communion with God?

But why need we specify? It is not one, but every branch of Christian duty that suffers from this defect. Because of it we are straitened in every part, and all our interests drag heavily. *Here*, then, the remedy must be applied. Deliverance will never be vouchsafed to us except on one condition, — *our fidelity to God.* Thus saith the Lord: "Bring ye all the tithes into the storehouse, that there may be meat in mine house, and prove me now herewith, if I will not open you the windows of heaven, and pour you out a blessing, that there shall not be room enough to receive it."

Our *possessions* must be consecrated anew to God. They must be, *practically*, considered as not ours, but

God's. They *are* his. His are the gold and the silver and the cattle upon a thousand hills; and whatever is found in our hands is lent to us to occupy for the interests of the great Proprietor. This must be more generally felt and acknowledged. The whole property question needs to be reëxamined. It is but half understood. There are thousands of men in our churches who, notwithstanding all that is said of Christian stewardship, do not comprehend the alphabet of this doctrine. They plan, and toil, and accumulate, to pamper their passions, and never dream that they are embezzling the Lord's property. Accuse them of fraudulently appropriating to their own use the money or goods intrusted to their care and management by the *government*, or by a *company*, or an *individual*, and their quick resentment will show how clearly they discover the criminal character of such a transaction. Did they as clearly perceive the guilt involved in hoarding up the LORD'S goods, or appropriating them, to an unjustifiable extent, to their own use, would it be possible to silence the clamors of conscience, or carry an unblushing face in the sight of God or men? Surely there is guilt in the latter case as well as in the former. In neither case is there any real proprietorship. In the former it will be acknowledged there is none; on what ground can it be supposed to exist in the latter? Is it the fact that the property has been accumulated by active industry? It has been *but* accumulated; its elements were always in existence. They owe their origin to God; and by continuing them in existence he every moment asserts his right to them. Moreover, he imparted the ability and skill necessary to their collection and combination. Hence it is written, "Thou must remember the Lord thy God, for it is he that giveth thee power to get wealth:" and hence also we are cautioned against saying in our hearts, "my power, and the might of my own hand hath gotten me this wealth." Therefore all that which men call *their* property is really the *Lord's.* He has never transferred his title to it, but holds us strictly accountable for its use.

Would that it were universally and practically so considered. Would that every recollection of property were associated with the recollection of God as its supreme owner. How much of misdirected expenditure were then turned into channels of benevolence! How much wealth now wholly unavailable were consecrated to Christ's service!

When Oliver Cromwell visited Yorkminster Cathedral, in England, his attention was drawn to twelve statues of the apostles, in silver, which stood in their appropriate niches near the ceiling of one of the apartments. Looking upon them for a moment, he inquired, "Who are those fellows standing yonder?" And on being informed, he exclaimed, "Take them down, and let them go about doing good." Accordingly they were melted down and put into his treasury. So let a right sentiment as to Christian stewardship once obtain, and many a wealthy professor, as he surveyed his splendid establishment, would be constrained to convert his extravagant decorations and costly plate into money for the Lord's treasury; thus sending them forth on the sublime errand of doing good. Nor the wealthy alone, but all classes, were this sentiment to obtain, would join in the glorious reform, until the present system of selfishness were entirely broken up, and the cause of benevolence made to wear an aspect altogether new. But that which is most necessary, nay, is absolutely essential to the best interests of all that is sacred, is a renewed and entire consecration of the *heart* to him who claims our supreme love.

As has been already intimated, the church of Christ has become extensively secularized. Once it was indeed a peculiar people. It required no reference to written documents to ascertain whether a man were a Christian. Every adherent to the true faith was a "living epistle known and read of all men;" and all "took knowledge" of him that he "had been with Jesus."

But alas, how different in our day! "How is the gold become dim! how is the most fine gold changed!" The line which should clearly divide the church from the world has become indistinct, and the two classes would almost appear to be blended in one. Their pursuit of the vanities of earth appears equally earnest and unremitting; and their love of self and the pleasures of life equally strong. It would seem that the mass of professors are trying the fearful experiment of determining with how little true godliness a man may get to heaven. There is not growth and development in the piety of Christians generally. Instead of "growing in grace" from the point of their conversion onward, there is oftentimes a satisfaction with present attainments, if not an absolute retrogression. Instead of "being filled with the spirit," the holy influence is wellnigh quenched with the tide of worldliness.

There is not enough of religion in the church. It is not only deficient in character but in *measure.* It was the aspiration of the apostle that his brethren might be "able to comprehend with all saints what is the length and breadth and depth and height of the love of God, and know that love which passeth knowledge, *and be filled with all the fulness of God.*"

And it is for want of this *fulness of God*, that we most suffer. We may talk about the modes and methods and measures and machinery of doing good, and render them never so perfect; yet, after all, while so deficient in goodness ourselves, we shall impart little of it to others. The sun is *full* of heat and light; and it asks no questions as to *how* it shall do good, but is perpetually pouring out its golden flood. The spring that sparkles at the foot of the hill is *full;* and asking leave of no one, is forever welling forth its sweet waters. So the Christian, if only *full* of the love of God and man, were shedding around him benign influences *as a natural result.* He could not help doing good. Regardless as to the mode and time and place, he were everywhere, and by all means, in season and out of season, dropping blessings from his beneficent heart and hand.

This exuberance of piety accounts, in a great measure, for the success of the early Christians. If the papal hierarchy had been in existence when the conversion of the Roman empire was first proposed, and had undertaken the work, much time had been spent in the adjustment of forms, in graduating official titles and robes and ranks, and in settling upon well-concerted plans of operation. But instead of all this, the disciples, each for himself, first drew near to the Great Fountain of life and love, in earnest prayer, and ceased not until he was filled with the Holy Ghost, and power from on high. Then went they forth to herald the tidings of the great salvation. They went from the spontaneous and irrepressible power of religion in their hearts. Theirs was the experience of the prophet Jeremiah: "His word was in mine heart *as a burning fire shut up in my bones, and I was weary with forbearing, and I could not stay.*" Thus were they possessed by the one great fact of the gospel — the death of Christ for man's salvation — and they broke that message upon the ear of whomsoever they met, *because it was the outbursting of a spontaneous and irrepressible force.* It is a piety such as this that is requisite. Always important, it is now indispensable. It is essential, not only to the saving of unconverted men, but also to the saving of Christians from the corrupting influences by which they are beset.

The perils to which many are exposed, simply from commerce and wealth, are imminent in the extreme. Men are everywhere making haste to get rich. Not content to plod for wealth, the spirit of speculation and bold adventure is abroad; and all branches of trade and pursuit are thrown open to the most unrestricted competition. The desire for gain is stimulated to the highest pitch, and never was it so largely successful as it has been within a few years past. We are fast becoming a wealthy people. It is announced that the real estate of the single city of New York has already risen to the enormous amount of nearly five hundred millions of dollars, the increase of one year being estimated at eighty-seven millions of dollars, and the increase of extravagant expenditure is even still greater. This may be an extreme case; but who has failed to observe, that in all parts of the country, and in all pursuits, there has been, of late, an unprecedented progress in the accumulation of property? What this nation will become at the present and prospective rate of progress, it is impossible to conjecture. But one thing is certain from all this: Christian character is to be subjected to a most severe ordeal. What will be the result? Will men acquire much of this world's goods, and yet set their affections, not upon these things on the earth, but upon those things which are in heaven? Will Mammon stalk abroad among us, and Christians still refuse to bow down before his shrine? Will fashion, pleasure, and preferment everywhere allure, and yet Christians stand firm? Will successful enterprise carry men to elevated points in social position, and yet they retain the sweet simplicity and humility of their first love? Will they gain money and not *love* money? Will they become rich and not fall into temptations, and many a foolish and hurtful lust? Ah! these are questions of momentous interest! How does the heart of the true disciple ache and throb as he contemplates them! How involuntary, and yet how earnest his prayer, God save them from the impending evil! And what is our hope in these perilous times, except a well-developed piety in the Christian church! Only let there be the indwelling of Christ,

— the fulness of God, — the breadth and depth of sanctified affection that characterized the early disciples, and all is well, while without it all is lost.

We have alluded to but one class of corrupting influences to which Christians of the present time are peculiarly exposed. It is not needful to recur to others, to enforce the argument which they afford for a more entire consecration to God. But let it be observed, that this is not only necessary to enable the church to resist evil, but also that she may be able to subdue the world to Christ. There must be power within, before there is impression without. We shall poorly succeed in inducing others to yield up their hearts to God, until we have fully yielded up our own hearts. Or, as another has observed, how can we expect to reclaim the world to Christ, when large tracts of our own character are unreclaimed; when the most fruitful and cherished tracts within us are pagan tracts, where the objects and idols of sense are worshipped?

Piety purifies and elevates the motives, directs and energizes the active powers, and gives solidity and strength to the whole moral being. Were an adequate consecration generally to obtain, existing errors and imperfections in the church would not only disappear without further controversy, but, with no addition to her present numerical strength, her efforts for the world's salvation would be incalculable and irresistible. And until this does obtain, no relief will be found for difficulties and perplexities under which the cause of the Redeemer now labors. Unconverted men will still live unconverted around us, — our benevolent enterprises will be still embarrassed for want of funds, and the nations will still sit in darkness.

Timely and true are the words of one who has said, "never will the church meet her responsibilities until her children, bursting asunder the shackles that bind them, and rising out of the slough of earthliness in which they are sunk, come up to that high measure of evangelical sanctification which the voice of Scripture and the exigencies of a dying world alike demand of them. There is a moral omnipotence in holiness. Argument may be resisted, persuasion and entreaty may be scorned. The thrilling appeals and monitions of the pulpit, set forth with all the vigor of logic, and all the glow of eloquence, may be evaded or disregarded. But the exhibition of exalted piety, has a might which nothing can withstand; it is truth embodied; it is the gospel burning in the hearts, beaming from the eyes, breathing from the lips, and preaching in the lives of its votaries. No sophistry can elude it, no conscience can ward it off; no bosom wears a mail that can brave the energy of its attack. It speaks in all languages, in all climes, and to all phases of our nature. It is universal, invincible; and clad in immortal panoply, goes on from victory to victory.

"Let Zion, through all her departments, but reach this elevated point, and how rapid and triumphant would be her progress! With what overpowering demonstration would her tidings be attended! What numerous and ever-flowing channels would pour into her treasury the requisite means; and what hosts of her consecrated sons would stand forth, to publish on every shore the mandates of her king! And how richly would the showers of divine influence be shed down, quickening into life the seed which she scatters, filling the desolate places with verdure and joy, and changing this blighted earth into the garden of the Lord!"*

And let it be also observed, that this high degree of consecration is to be gained only in connection with earnest effort for its attainment. The truth here indicated is often lost sight of; a circumstance which renders it more important that it be well considered. How little time is spent in the cultivation of piety, by the majority of Christians! How few and feeble are their efforts for greater attainments in holiness! How little hungering and thirsting after righteousness! How little watching and praying, and laboring and striving to become more completely sanctified in heart and life!

This is not in keeping with the analogy of things; for though every good gift is from above, yet it comes not to us without exertion on our part. It is most certainly true of the glorious gift of sanctification. Dr. Jonathan Edwards, in a letter to a pious young lady, advises her "to keep as great a strife and earnestness in religion" as if she knew herself to be in a state of nature, and were seeking conversion. He says of converts, "they ought not to be the less watchful, laborious, and earnest in the whole work of religion, but the more so, for they are under infinitely greater obligations." And he reminds her that for want of this, many persons, in a few months after their conversion, have begun to lose their sweet and

---

* Rev. George B. Ide, D. D.

lively sense of spiritual things, and to grow cold and dark; whereas if they had imitated the apostle (Phil. 3:12) their path would have been as a "shining light that shines more and more unto the perfect day."

And by reference to the Scriptures we shall find that those of ancient times who were eminent for piety, became and continued such not without a constant struggle. Hence the frequent allusions to crucifying the flesh, and mortifying the lusts thereof; and to seeking after God, oftentimes with protracted humiliation and fasting and prayer. Hence also the language of an apostle, "This one thing I do, forsaking those things which are behind, and reaching forth unto those things which are before, I press toward the mark for the prize of the high calling of God in Christ Jesus." And again; "So fight I, not as one that beateth the air; but I keep my body under, (literally, I strike my body under the eye, alluding to the blows of the pugilist,) and bring it into subjection: lest that by any means, when I have preached to others, I myself should be a castaway."

So also of men of modern times. Whitefield attained the measure of sanctification which so enhanced his usefulness, by a painful process. "He fasted himself sick; and denied himself in dress to such a degree, that the young nobleman who gave him a certain amount at the University, dismissed him for shame of so shabby a groom." That there may have been somewhat of the legal spirit in this, is very probable; and yet it shows how earnestly he sought after that communion with God which gave him such power among men.

Payson, who moved about on the earth while he lived, "like a flame of fire," affords a striking example in proof of this position. He prayed without ceasing; studying his theology on his knees, with an open Bible, and a pleading of the promises; and was so rigid in watchings and fastings as to cause his friends to be justly alarmed for his safety. Turn to his diary, and mark the following as specimens of many entrances: —

"March 26. — Spent the day in fasting and prayer," etc.

"March 31. — Spent this day in fasting, but not in prayer; for I could not put up a single petition. Was entirely deserted and ready to say, Surely it is in vain to seek after God," etc.

"April 7. — In fasting and prayer was favored with much of a spirit of supplication," etc.

"April 22. — Spent this day in fasting and prayer. At first stupid; but soon God was pleased to lift up the light of his countenance upon me," etc.

"May 1, 1807. — Having set apart this day for fasting and prayer, preparatory to the celebration of the Lord's supper, I arose early and sought the divine presence," etc.

"May 5. — Spent this day in the woods, in fasting and prayer, with a view to obtain mortification of my abominable pride and selfishness," etc.

"June 26. — Much favored. Felt insatiable desires after holiness, and that I might spend every moment of future life to the divine glory," etc.*

We have another example in Timothy W. Lester,

* See his Memoir published by Tract Society.

in whose biography sentences like the following often meet the eye: —

"Spent yesterday to some extent as a day of fasting, self-examination, and prayer. This exercise seems always beneficial to both body and soul."

"After breakfast, I took to my study to spend the day in prayer and in searching the Scriptures." "By close self-examination, I discover that I am becoming less spiritual. The thought greatly distresses me. I cast myself at the feet of Jesus my Saviour, and cried for more grace. I went again and again to the mercy-seat. The Spirit helped my infirmity," etc.*

Alas, that this striving after holiness is so infrequent among the disciples of Christ! Alas, that they should allow themselves so little time for retirement and reflection.

> "Wisdom's self
> Oft seeks to sweet retired solitude;
> Where, with her best nurse, Contemplation,
> She plumes her feathers, and lets grow her wings."

It is not possible to detect all the causes that operate to this result. Doubtless, in many instances, it arises from losing sight of its necessity; sometimes from the absence of any desire for holiness, owing to a deadness of the affections, and a wicked departure from God. More frequently it is because the cares of the world too exclusively occupy the mind and exhaust the energies.

In many instances, it is to be feared that there is

---

* Memoir of Timothy W. Lester, by Rev. Isaac C. Beach.

little earnest effort for higher attainments in piety, from being satisfied with a mere superficial, outside religion. Formalism has always been the great foe of a pure Christianity. There were those of old who had the form of godliness, but not its power; and even true Christians, especially in our day, are in danger of substituting an outward attention to the claims of philanthropy and religion, for a deep, personal experience of its life and power within. The number of benevolent enterprises which have recently sprung into being, and which are the glory of the age, increase this danger of neglecting the *heart-work*, upon which these very enterprises are dependent for success. There are so many "Societies," and "Boards," and "Conventions," the importance of whose efficient operations and liberal support, must of necessity be often urged upon the churches, that we are in danger of imbibing the sentiment that these are the *only* things of importance; and that, when we have done our proportion for their adequate support and encouragement, we may rest satisfied as if all were attained. Thus the *inner work* of the closet, and the individual's own bosom, is left undone.

This, as above intimated, is neglecting the very basis on which the whole superstructure of our systems of benevolence, if successful, must rest; for, as some one has observed, *it is a principle of divine appointment, that personal piety is the only proper basis of relative usefulness.*

Our Saviour spent much time in solitude. Forty days were passed in fasting and prayer and personal conflict with the adversary, previous to his entrance upon the public ministry; and special mention is made of his afterward retiring, on at least three different occasions, for solemn private and protracted prayer. "And in the morning, rising up a great while before day, he went out and departed into a solitary place, and there prayed." Mark 1: 35. "He went out into a mountain to pray, and continued all night in prayer." Luke 6: 12. "And when he had sent the multitude away, he went up into a mountain to pray; and when the evening was come, he was there alone." Matt. 14: 23.

"Cold mountains and the midnight air
Witnessed the fervor of his prayer;
The desert his temptations knew,
His conflict and his victory too."

And in proof of the necessity of frequent retirement for meditation and prayer, in order to great attainments in grace, we have not only our Lord's example, but his express precept: "Enter into thy closet, and when thou hast shut thy door, pray to thy Father which is in secret." Matt. 6: 6.

But how little time is spent in this manner by Christians generally! Perhaps at no previous period so little as at the present. And this is only indicative of a general fact, — the prevalence of an exterior rather than an interior religion. There is foreign work, and home work, — all kinds of *out-door* work, — but alas for the work *within!* Our Lord's admonition is here in point: "These ought ye to have done, but not to leave the other undone."

The piety of the age needs to be driven back again to the home-altar, and the closet; not, indeed, to remain there; but to be renewed and replenished from on high, that it may come forth with more purity and depth and strength. First attend to the heart, and then let the hands be filled with work. In this case all will be well. There will be both piety and activity. "Our piety will give activity to our benevolence, and, in return, our benevolence will invigorate our piety." But reversing this divine order, disappointment and disaster will be the inevitable result. What is gained in surface will be lost in depth; and the expenditures exceeding the receipts, we shall become morally bankrupt. Hence the propriety of the admonition of another: "The more active the church is in the way of proselyting, the more devoted it should be in the way of piety. Without this, even the present missionary ardor instead of being as the light-house of the world, will be but as a bonfire upon the heights of Zion, a transient blaze, which will soon burn itself out, and yield no permanent illumination. Here, then, must be our starting point; to begin anywhere else is to begin in the middle. It is one of Satan's deep devices to call off the attention of the church from its own state, to the condition of the world without and around her. . . . The spirit of holy zeal which is so active, — yes, even this, for the want of watchfulness, care, and earnest prayer, may become a snare and a mischief to personal godliness. We have need to take care that the reproach be not brought against us, that, while we have kept the vineyards of others, our own we have not kept; that our zeal has been maintained, not by our religion, but at the expense of it; that our ardor is not the natural putting forth of the vital energies of the tree, in branches, leaves, and fruit, but an excrescence upon it, which draws to itself the sap and impoverishes the genuine produce."

Our conclusion, then, is, that in point of consecration to the Lord, there should be an immediate and general return to the piety of primitive times. Let Christians place before them an elevated standard of holiness. Let them not wickedly abuse the doctrine that sin, to some extent, will cleave to us while we abide in the flesh, by making it an excuse for remaining contented without that perfect holiness to which we should constantly aim. Though they may never here attain to it, yet let them strive after a complete conformity to Christ.

It is worthy of observation, that there is a correct sentiment in the churches as to the needful consecration of heart and life in *ministers* and *missionaries*, who are *expected* to be men of eminent piety. And such they most certainly ought to be. As pressing as is the demand for more ministers, there is a call, louder than all others, demanding *more piety in* the ministry. But is it less imperative as regards private Christians? Is it not equally true of them, that they are bought with a price, and being not their own, are bound to glorify God in their bodies and spirits which are his? Let all the members of our churches, then, both ministers and laymen, arise and with one heart return unto God, and seek a fresh anointing from on high.

As aids in the blessed undertaking, let every means of grace be faithfully employed. Let there be more study of the sacred truths of the Bible. For the doctrines of revelation are the life of the soul, the foundation of all experimental and practical religion.

A man's creed influences his conduct. Opinions are the seeds of actions. The better exemplification of the doctrines of the gospel in the Christian's life, must be the result of a clearer view, and a consequent more realizing persuasion of those doctrines. It has been well and truly said, that "the basis of a vigorous and intelligent piety can be laid only in correct Christian doctrine. Those great truths which the gospel requires us to believe contain the reasons and the source of all the peculiar traits of character which it requires to possess. Displace one of them from the system, or misstate and pervert it, and you give a new turn to the entire Christian life. Neglect them wholly, and your piety withers like a tree severed from its root, or is driven by the gusts of enthusiasm like a paper kite cut loose from its string."

There can be no true religion without some knowledge of God's law, and man's guilt, and Christ's sacrifice. As well might we conceive of a building without a foundation, as of religion without doctrinal knowledge; for the duties of religion are all founded upon its doctrines, and from them all the motives to a godly life are derived. And beside, it is *divine truth* that the Spirit employs in the work of sanctification. "Sanctify them through thy truth; thy word is truth."

It does not admit of a doubt that the very general lack of a full and distinct apprehension of the great and glorious doctrines of the Bible is one main cause of the existing defects in Christian character. The Bible in our day is too much a neglected book. The knowledge that is possessed of it, even among intelligent Christians, is exceedingly superficial. This holy volume has been crowded out by the pressure of publications of a light and ephemeral character. These latter books must be read,—the daily and weekly papers must be read,—but the Bible, and those solid books defining and illustrating its precious doctrines, are by many ignored and slighted and forgotten. Is it strange that their piety is of a negative and unfruitful character?

And it is worthy of serious inquiry here, Whether the exclusion from many pulpits of thorough doctrinal preaching has not contributed greatly to a superficial religion? Is it not seldom that we now have presented from the pulpit a clear statement and a forcible elucidation of the fundamental truths of the gospel? When preached at all, is it not incidentally and feebly, rather than in that clear and forcible manner which awakens the feelings of the human heart in view of the objects they present, and which tends to humble the pride of man and exalt God upon the throne as the rightful and sovereign Disposer of all?

Is there not, then, an imperious necessity for a more general and distinct apprehension of the truths of revelation, in order to a revival of primitive piety? Those great fundamental doctrines,—the divine Trinity,—the fall and depravity of man,—his just condemnation by the divine law,—the atonement of Christ,—regeneration by the Holy Spirit, justification by faith in Christ,—God's sovereignty in man's salvation, and eternal rewards and punishments,—the thorough exposition and inculcation of which have secured for Scotland the title of "the vanguard of Christ's army," and for New England an equally desirable elevation in this land, need to be more frequently and thoroughly discussed and better understood.

How else shall the churches ward off the insidious and open assaults of rationalism and traditionalism and superstition and fanaticism? A clear and scriptural presentation of the doctrines is "the true breakwater which *alone* can resist the billows of prevailing errors." And how shall the needful vigor and maturity of the churches be restored and maintained, except in connection with the more uninterrupted circulation through all the members of their life's blood which is composed of these doctrines received into the heart as actual living principles? *

Let there be, therefore, more of the daily searching of the Scriptures,—more of that meditation on God's law and truth, which causes the Christian to be like a tree planted by the rivers of water, that bringeth forth his fruit in his season, and whose leaf shall not wither. And with this study of the word of the living God, let there be a return to those old devotional and doctrinal works on which was fed the piety of our fathers, productions which, though not excelled in intrinsic merit by those of modern date, have, nevertheless, fallen into comparative disuse; works such as Taylor's Holy Living and Dying,—Bunyan's Pilgrim's Progress,—Baxter's Saint's Rest,—the works of President Edwards, Bellamy, Hopkins, Andrew Fuller, Dwight, and others of like instructive character.

---

* See an able discussion of this subject in Tract No. 1 of the series by the Congregational Board of Publication.

Let the sanctuary be frequented with more regularity and purity of motive, and, above all, let there be more of deep humiliation and prayer, — prayer in the social circle, at the family altar, and particularly in the closet, where the exercise should always be accompanied with devout meditation and deep self-abasement. So let there be a rekindling of the "first love;" a closer walk with God; a consecration such as the necessities of the age, and the word of God, imperatively enjoin. Thus shall be experienced the blessings of the day foretold of the prophet, when "there shall be upon the bells of the horses HOLINESS UNTO THE LORD;" and Zion, clothed in garments of salvation, and robes of righteousness, shall reflect abroad the light of heaven, and become the admiration of the whole earth.

And, finally, dear reader, what is the measure of *your* consecration to God? Are you a minister of the gospel? Then *your* piety determines, in no small degree, the piety of the flock over which the Holy Ghost has made you overseer, and of the whole community where your influence is exerted. If a particular church is to attain a high degree of spirituality, its pastor must first become spiritually minded; for how can one inspire in others the desire of an object concerning which he is himself indifferent? "It is the scintillation of his own zeal, flying off from his own glowing heart, and falling upon their souls, which kindles in them the fire which burns in himself." How responsible, then, is your position! Luther, it is said, trembled every time he entered the pulpit. And well he might. Well might one tremble from the single consideration that a whole congregation of immortal souls were moulding and forming the type of their piety from that of his own! Such is *your* position; and hence the vast importance of watching over your own soul, as well as the souls of others, and so habitually dwelling upon the mount of communion that your face shall shine with the reflected light of God's countenance, as did that of Moses.

Are you a private member of the church, and engaged in the secular pursuits of life? It is well that you often and solemnly propose to yourself questions like these: "Am I toiling for myself, or for my Maker?" "This active mind, and this body, with its feet and hands and mouth, its bones and sinews, have I devoted them wholly to God?" "I have this day been before God," says President Edwards, "and have given myself — all that I am and have — to God; so that I am in no respect my own. I can challenge no right in myself; in this understanding, this will, these affections. Neither have a right to this body, or any of its members; no right to this tongue, these hands, these feet, these eyes, these ears; I have given myself clean away." Is this the measure of *your* personal consecration? If you have children, have you truly devoted them to the Lord and his service? And is this true of the property which you have been enabled to acquire, whether it be less or more?

When the Karen convert, Ko-chet-thing, was in America, a few friends of missions gave him small sums of money, amounting in all to some forty or fifty dollars. After it had been exchanged for Spanish dollars, on the eve of his return to his own country, he one day held up the bag containing the amount, apparently exulting in his treasure. A friend asked him what use he intended to make of the money, supposing that he would probably purchase various articles as keepsakes to carry home to his kindred. He had, however, set it apart for building a school-house among the Karens; and to the innocent inquiry, looking up with tears of gratitude in his eyes, he replied, in his broken English, "This no me money, this Jesus Christ's money," — "this no me money, this Jesus Christ's money."

Christian reader, — you who have sat under the sound of the gospel from your youth up,— have you as thoroughly and as *practically* learned the great doctrine of *stewardship* as this convert from heathenism? No matter what your standing in the church, you are entreated to look well to this matter. Your outward profession may be very fair, while there is a covetous disposition within. Apply the proper tests. They are such as these. Does your love of money terminate upon yourself? Do you desire riches that you may gratify your pride, or your inclinations toward accumulating a fortune for yourself or your heirs, or procuring worldly ease and preferment among men? Then the desire for gain is unholy. Are you a reluctant giver? Do you grudge what you give, and wish that you were not compelled to give it? Are you inclined to shun the duty of liberality if possible? and if not possible, are you impelled to withhold from charity all that you can withhold, and yet not be suspected of meanness, and a narrow, illiberal spirit? If this be so, you are guilty of covetousness. And so, also, if this passion for property reigns with so much power as to displace the supremacy of God from the mind. Nor let your self-examination terminate with the points already mentioned, but carry it forward with special reference to the degree of your love of Christ, and hatred of sin in every form. Are you able to adopt the language of the Psalmist as applied to the Redeemer? "Whom have I in heaven but thee? and there is none upon earth that I desire beside thee." And with regard to any act that might displease the Lord, can you enter into the feeling of Count Godomar, who was accustomed to say, "that he feared nothing in the world more than *sin;* and that whatever liberties he had formerly taken, *he would rather now submit to be torn to pieces by wild beasts, than knowingly or willingly commit any sin against God?*"

CHAPTER IV.

A WANT OF SELF-DENIAL FOR CHRIST — A THIRD GRAND DEFECT IN THE PIETY WHICH NOW PREVAILS.

What is Self-denial? — Why required. — How exercised. — Practised by God's People in all Ages. — Still demanded. — Unless suffered with Him, not reign with Him. — The Duty explicitly enjoined. — A great Law of the Christian Religion. — Just as much Religion as Self-denial. — Not practised to requisite extent at the present Time. — Reluctance of Parents to give Children to Mission Service. — Limited benevolent Contributions. — General Style of Living. — Conformity to the World. — Ungodly Men give Laws to the Church. — The Usurpation indorsed. — The Evil on the increase. — Calamitous Results. — A Return to the Simplicity of former Days a pressing Necessity. — Not safe for God's Children to follow after the World. — The Self-sacrificing Spirit waits a Resurrection. — Incentives to Self-denial. — The constraining Power of Love. — Individual Application of the Subject.

In the preceding chapter we were led to consider the subject of an adequate consecration to God. Now it will be obvious upon the least reflection, that the entire surrender which it involves, is directly at variance with the natural inclinations of the human heart; and can, therefore, be effected only in connection with a disregard of self, and a supreme regard for the Divine will. Hence the necessity of *self-denial*, a feature of Christian character which is worthy of the most careful consideration.

But what *is* self-denial? Simply the denial of one's self; the forbearing to gratify one's own appetites or desires. The self-denial which the gospel enjoins, may be more fully defined as "the subjection of our personal ease and tastes and conveniences, our comforts and time and possessions, to the will of Christ, for his glory and human good." And why is it requisite? That true Christians may be distinguished from those that are false; that the unbelieving world may be convinced of our sincerity, and of the reality of our blessed religion; that, by resisting and overcoming that which is evil, we may be elevated in the scale of being; as well as that heaven's joys may be. sweetened, on account of earth's trials.

Let us further inquire, How is it to be exercised? Not in rejecting the lawful use of God's creatures,— not in reducing one's self to voluntary and comfortless poverty,—not in burying one's self in retirement, and macerating the body, and wasting the energies "in idle contemplations and dreamy raptures," — not in being careless of life and health and property,—but in renouncing such pleasures. profits, comforts, connections, or practices as God commands us to renounce, and to the extent to which he commands it. The understanding must be so far denied as that we shall not lean upon it, independent of divine instruction. The will must be denied so far as it opposes the will of God,—the affections, when they become inordinate,—the gratification of the members of the body, when out of their due course,—the honors of the world and praise of men, when they become a snare,—worldly emoluments, when to be obtained in an unlawful way, or when standing in opposition to religion and usefulness,--

friends and relatives, so far as they oppose the truth, and would influence us to oppose it, — our property and our temporal comforts, yea, life itself, if called for in the service of Christ.*

And, once more, let us observe the *spirit* in which we are to exercise self-denial: which is not one of strife or vainglory, or out of a desire to seek the praise of men, or secure to ourselves the favor of God; but in the spirit of faith, and of love, and of a sound mind.

We are now prepared to remark, that the people of God in all ages have been called to the exercise of this self-sacrificing spirit, — Abel, in rendering himself liable to his brother's wrath, and finally in the loss of his life, — Abraham, in leaving his country and his father's house, and in the sacrifice of his son Isaac, — Joseph, in bringing upon himself the displeasure of his master, and in being cast into the king's prison, — Moses, in forsaking the pleasures of sin, and the riches of Egypt, to suffer affliction and reproach with God's people, — Daniel, in being thrust into the den of lions, and the three worthies into the fiery furnace, for their adherence to the Divine commands, — and others of their times, in being put to death, or afflicted and tormented for the truth's sake.

And so of the early disciples of Christ. They were left to no conjecture as to the results of espousing the cause of the Nazarene. At the dawn of his ministry, those who would follow him were admonished that it would involve sacrifices of the most try-

---

* See Buck's Theological Dictionary.

ing nature. "The foxes have holes, and the birds of the air have nests; but the Son of man hath not where to lay his head." "Follow me; and let the dead bury their dead." They must *leave all*, and expect nothing but revilings and persecutions, perhaps death. But the greatness of their sacrifices did not excel the readiness with which they were made. Their hearts overflowing with "the first love," they lost sight of themselves, and thought only of Christ. Witness the case of the four fishermen — the first chosen of his disciples. Called by their Lord, they immediately forsook all that they had hitherto valued and loved, and followed him. It was more than abandoning their *property*, which might have been considerable. As Kitto remarks, it was a forsaking of the place, the homes around which, for them, all the charities of life were gathered, — of the friends and neighbors with whom they had been accustomed to associate, and of the relations in whom their hearts were delighted. It was an abandonment of the habits of life to which they had been used, and of the occupation in which alone they were skilled, and which furnished their subsistence. And this, not to attach themselves to one who was rich or great, or who could or did hold out to them any worldly advantages, — but to one who was as poor as themselves, and one with whom they were often to suffer peril, hunger, and thirst, and who could not assure them of a place where to lay their heads.*

And this incident is but illustrative of a general fact in regard to the primitive disciples; they made

* Life of our Lord, p. 244.

but little account of the treasures of this life. The love of *money* they knew nothing of. If the poor brethren required aid, what was possessed by others, was laid at the feet of the apostles for distribution; and if, through violence, their property was wrested from them, they "took joyfully the spoiling of their goods." In charity, "their deep poverty abounded to the riches of their liberality," and their gifts extended even "beyond their power." With them the question was not, as in our day, "How much shall I give?" but rather, "How much may I withhold?" Indeed, they gave the *whole* of what they gained. All of it was honestly dedicated to God, — they did not esteem it *theirs;* and were only anxious lest they should err in appropriating too much to their own use. Nor did their self-denial extend to property alone, but to their *lives* even. The teachings of their Master had animated them with a spirit of entire self-devotement; and they literally feared not "them that kill the body, but are not able to kill the soul," but rather "Him which is able to destroy both soul and body in hell." When brought before councils, they took no thought of what they should say; and, instead of recoiling from scourgings and imprisonments for Christ's sake, they absolutely rejoiced "that they were counted worthy to suffer shame for his name."

Witness the heroic Paul, as his friends, in tears, stood about him and entreated him not to go up to Jerusalem, on an occasion when it was known that he would suffer harm: "What mean ye?" he exclaims, "to weep and to break mine heart? for I am ready, not to be bound only, but also to *die* at

Jerusalem for the name of the Lord Jesus." On another occasion, he declares that it is his earnest hope "that Christ shall be magnified in" his "body, whether it be by life or by death;" adding, "for me to live is Christ; and to die is gain." And again, says he, "If I be offered upon the sacrifice and service of your faith, I joy and rejoice with you all." And, at last, in sight of the instruments of his death, with holy boldness he exclaims, "I am now ready to be offered." The time of his departure had come; and God permitted him to seal his testimony with his blood,—a privilege vouchsafed not to him alone, for, according to the general belief, all the apostles save one, died by the bloody hand of fierce persecution.

It is, moreover, interesting to observe how extensively this spirit of self-sacrificing devotion prevailed among the Christians of the first few centuries succeeding the apostolic age. Some perilled their lives in going forth to all places with the message of salvation; while others sacrificed nearly the whole of their property to furnish means for evangelizing the heathen around them; and others still, contributed to this purpose the entire avails of their labor. Of one man it is recorded, that "he sold himself as a slave to a heathen family, to get access to them for their conversion; and for years cheerfully endured the labor and condition of a slave, till he succeeded with the whole family, and took his liberty from the gratitude of the converts." The same, it is said, "on a visit to Sparta, again entered himself as a slave, in the family of the governor of Sparta, and served two years, and again succeeded in his design." What thought such men of self-indulgence? What cared they for life, if called to surrender it in the Master's service?

Hear their language: "We say we are Christians, and we say it to the whole world, under the hand of the executioner. In the midst of all the tortures you can heap upon us to make us recant; torn and mangled, and covered with our own blood, we still cry out as loud as we are able, We are Christians. Call us by what names you please; fill our flesh with fagots to set us on fire, yet let me tell you, that when we are thus begirt and dressed about with fire, we are in our most illustrious apparel. These are our victorious palms and robes of glory; and, mounted on our funeral pile, we feel ourselves as in a triumphant chariot. We conquer when we die, and the spoils of that victory is eternal life." "What you reproach us with as stubbornness, is the best means of proselyting the world. For who has not been struck with the sight of such fortitude, and from thence pushed on to look into the reason of it? And who ever looked well into our religion, but embraced it? *And who ever embraced it, but was willing to die for it?*" "The more you mow us down, the thicker we rise; the Christian blood you spill is like the seed you sow; it springs from the earth and fructifies the more." "Therefore, all the refinements of your cruelty can effect nothing, or rather they have brought over persons to this sect: our number augments the more you persecute us. The blood of Christians is the seed they sow. Your philosophers, who exhort to the endurance of pain and death, make not so many disciples as the Christians through their deeds."

In language like this did they protest their readiness to suffer and die for the truth which they had embraced. And for it did they die, by hecatombs, while, in the very deed, their blood became the seed of the church.

But the question may arise, Are the disciples of Christ in our day and in Christian lands, called upon to exercise any considerable degree of self-denial? Was it not a necessity peculiar to primitive times? We fear it is often so considered. Doubtless, the *same form* of self-denial is not in all times and places required; but it is highly erroneous to suppose that because the bloody persecutions for righteousness' sake, which the early Christians suffered, have now, to a great extent, abated, therefore the necessity for the exercise of this virtue no longer exists.

The true people of God, if in character and life they meet the divine requirement, will always be, as they have always been, a *suffering* people. Christ is their great *example* in *suffering*, as well as in other things. He *himself suffered.* He himself has furnished us with the highest illustrations of a heroic denial of self for the good of others. He saw our moral pollution, but turned not away from us in disgust. "There is not a wretch now wallowing in the deepest mire of sin, who is so vile and low in our eyes, as we all were in the eyes of infinite purity. Yet the more wretched we were, the more did he feel for us." He saw the full measure of duty and of trial that awaited him, but recoiled not at the sight. He listened not to the voices of ten thousand times ten thousands of bright angels that stood about him, but only to the sad moan that ascended up from the abode of the guilty sons of men. He divested himself of his glory, and hastened to the rescue. He is born of woman, made under the law, that he might redeem us who were under the law. He chooses poverty; is dependent upon the charity of his friends for the sandals on his feet, the garments which he wears, the food which he eats, and the place where he may repose his weary head. He is "a man of sorrows, and acquainted with grief." "He is despised and rejected of men;" and at length "is brought as a lamb to the slaughter, and as a sheep before the shearers is dumb, so openeth he not his mouth." "He is wounded for our transgressions," "bruised for our iniquities," and "cut off out of the land of the living." *And all this for us*,—all this for his *enemies*,—"the just for the unjust."

O *this* is self-denial! This is suffering,—suffering that *others* need *not* suffer. And in this suffering he has left an example for his followers *in all time.* Says the apostle to the Gentiles, in his letter to the Philippians, "*Let this mind be in you*, which was also in Christ Jesus; who being in the form of God, thought it not robbery to be equal with God; but made himself of no reputation, and took upon him the form of a servant, and was made in the likeness of men; and being found in fashion as a man, he humbled himself, and became obedient unto death, even the death of the cross." And says Peter, "For even hereunto were ye called; because *Christ also suffered for us, leaving us an example, that ye should follow his steps.*" Observe: "He also suffered, LEAVING US AN EXAMPLE, *that ye should* FOLLOW HIS STEPS." Christ is therefore to be followed *in sufferings.*

"The Son of God goes forth to war,
A kingly crown to gain.
His blood-red banner streams afar;
Who follows in his train?
Who best can drink his cup of woe,
Triumphant over pain;
Who patient bears his cross below,
He follows in his train."

Paul declares concerning his brethren, that unto them "it is given in the behalf of Christ, not only to believe on him, but also *to suffer for his sake;*" and to his son Timothy he writes, "be thou partaker of the *afflictions* of the gospel." Indeed, *suffering* with Christ is made a *condition* of reigning with him. "If children, then heirs; heirs of God, and joint-heirs with Christ; IF SO BE *that we suffer with him, that we may be also glorified together.*" And let the language of our Lord upon this subject, contained in Matt. 10: 37, 38, and Luke 9: 23–25. 14: 25–35, be specially observed.

In the last-mentioned passage it is written that "there went great multitudes with him; and he turned and said unto them, If any man come to me, and hate not his father, and mother, and wife, and children, and brethren, and sisters, yea, and his own life also, he CANNOT BE MY DISCIPLE. And whosoever doth not *bear his cross*, and come after me, cannot be my disciple." And after enforcing the importance of *counting the cost* before determining to follow Christ, by allusion to a man who is about to build a tower, or a king to make war with a powerful rival, it is added, "So likewise, whosoever he be of you that *forsaketh not all that he hath*, he cannot be my disciple."

The occasion upon which the language in Luke 9: 23–25 was spoken, was the open avowal by Christ of his approaching sufferings and death; and the consequent trials to which his followers would be subjected. On this occasion it is written that "he said unto them all, If any man will come after me, let him deny himself, and take up his cross daily, and follow me. For whosoever will save his life shall lose it; but whosoever will lose his life for my sake, the same shall save it. For what is a man advantaged, if he gain the whole world, and lose himself, or be a castaway?" The record in Matt. 10: 37, etc., runs thus: "He that loveth father or mother more than me; and he that loveth son or daughter more than me, is not worthy of me. And he that taketh not his cross, and followeth after me, is not worthy of me."

Consider well the import of these remarkable passages. There is little difficulty in understanding any particular expressions which they contain.

Bearing the cross is an allusion to the custom of the Romans, who compelled the criminal to bear his own cross to the place of execution; and "the figure expresses with great energy the readiness which every Christian ought to exhibit, in enduring the severest reproaches, cruelties, and even the most ignominious death, for the sake of Christ."

The *hating of the father and the mother*, is evidently to be understood in a modified sense; intimating that every tie must be sacrificed, and every attachment disregarded, which comes into competition with Christ and his religion. *As compared with Christ*, the nearest relatives are to be hated; they must be *loved less* than Christ; the word *hate*, as in Gen. 29: 31. John 12: 25, and Rom. 9: 13, meaning to *love less*. Christ must be loved *supremely;* with a love so much transcending the love of kindred and friends, that the latter may be said to be no love at all. "*He that findeth his life shall lose it; and he that loseth his life for my sake, shall find it*," is a form of expression wherein the same word is used in different senses, in order to convey the sentiment with greater energy. The meaning may be thus expressed: "He that is anxious to save his *temporal* life, or his comfort or security here, shall lose eternal life; or shall fail of heaven. He that is willing to risk or lose, his comfort and life here, for my sake, shall find everlasting life, or shall be saved."

The forsaking of all that one hath, as a condition of discipleship, does not imply that Christians should, in all cases, leave their business and friends, and comforts and possessions; but rather that they *must be willing to do this*, prepared for even this trial and sacrifice, if the commandment and providence of God call them to it.

The great lesson which these Scriptures teach, is that of *self-denial for Christ*. This is made a *positive test* of the sincerity of one's profession. It is so in the things of this world. We judge of one's patriotism, not by his pretensions and professions, but by his willingness to sacrifice his own interests for his country's good. The depth of a parent's affection for his children, is best known by his readiness to toil and to suffer for their advantage. And you doubt the friendship of a neighbor, though professing to be never so friendly, if, when sick, or in destitution or distress, he is not willing to sacrifice his own gratifications for your comfort and relief. And so one cannot be a friend of Christ, a true disciple, unless he be willing to part with any thing and *every thing* for Christ. No matter what the object of affection may be, if he cannot and will not part with it, in case Christ requires it, and is to be glorified by his parting with it, he fails of possessing the qualifications of a true Christian. Christ must be preferred to every thing else. His will and pleasure must be our *supreme law.*

"Although the yearning bowels of a tender mother, and the gray hairs of an indulgent father," says Whitby, "should be pleaded as motives to induce me to break the least command of the holy Jesus; though the authority of civil, natural, or ecclesiastical superiors should tempt me to do what Christ forbids; though authority should allure me with proffers of the highest honors or rewards, or endeavor to affright me with the severest menaces; yet if all these considerations should prevail with me to gratify myself and them, by doing that which my own conscience and God's word assures me will be displeasing to my Saviour, or opposite to his commands; it is evident that I regard myself, or them, more than I do my Saviour, and therefore am unworthy of him, and cannot be sincerely his disciple."

Henry remarks that, "for the gains of a bargain, we must come up to its terms. Now the terms are settled. If religion be worth *any* thing, it is worth *every* thing; therefore all who believe its truth will come up to the price of it; and they will make it their business and bliss, will make every thing else yield to it. Those who like not Christ on these terms may leave him — at their peril. . . . The pearl of price is worth what we give for it. The terms are that we must prefer Christ; first before our nearest and dearest relations, *father* or *mother*, *son* or *daughter*. . . . Children must love their parents, and parents their children; but if they love them better than Christ, they are unworthy of him. As we must not be *deterred* from Christ by the hatred of our relations, so we must not be *drawn* from him by their love. Christians must be as Levi, who said to *his father, I have not seen him.* Secondly, before our ease and safety. We must *take up our cross and follow him*. . . . Thirdly, before *even life*. *He that findeth his life shall lose it*, — and he who thinks he has found it, when he has saved it by denying Christ, shall lose it in an eternal death."

And let it be observed that this self-denial is spoken of as a constant practice. The cross is to be borne "*daily*." "Great is the emphasis of this word," says Beza, "which indeed implies that as day succeeds day, so would one cross follow another." The divine hand has planted crosses all along life's pathway. We meet them at every step, nor are we at liberty to avoid them. We must "stoop to the burden," and as meekly, willingly, rejoicingly bear it, as Christ for us bore his cross. Sometimes the cross will consist in denying the cravings of pride, ambition, the love of money, ease, pleasure, — sometimes in blasting fair prospects for wealth and preferment, lest they prove detrimental to our piety, — sometimes in sacrificing endeared friendships, — sometimes in enduring contempt, and hardship, and abuse, and perhaps the loss of all things, for the sake of Christ, — but, in the spirit of him who for our sakes became poor, that we through his poverty might be made rich, we are to suffer and endure, counting it enough that the servant be as his Lord.

So also is the cross to be borne by *all* of Christ's followers. In this divine law of self-denial there is no limitation of time or individuals. The most comprehensive and explicit of the Scriptures referred to, was first spoken to "great multitudes," and by no just rule of interpretation can it be made to appear that these requirements are not in full force to-day, as truly as when they were first promulged. Were the Christians of primitive times, in obedience to these commands of Christ, required to "mortify their members which are on the earth," "denying ungodliness and every worldly lust?" to this duty are those of our own day equally bound. The sinful propensities, — those unlawful out-shootings of a partially sanctified nature, which, like noxious weeds, are ever springing up and sprouting afresh, — must be subdued and kept in subjection, or we are no more worthy of Christ, than were those of earlier days who were "drawn away of their own lusts and enticed." Were they required, by the spirit of this law, to "love not the world, neither the things that are in the world," and be "not conformed" to it, but "crucified to the world," while it was crucified to them? The same is required of us.

Any soul that is right with God is a crucified soul. It has undergone a painful death to worldly objects. And if it lives again in its attachment to earth, — if we find ourselves embracing the world, and loving it, — there is just occasion for alarm. The cross has been evaded. It has not been "daily" borne. It must be resumed; and we are not to rest satisfied until the inward crucifixion again takes place; until we have "no eye for the world's possessions, no ear for the world's applause, no tongue for the world's envious or useless conversation, no terror for the world's opposition;" and we experience Tauler's description of what it is to be inwardly crucified: "to cease entirely from the life of self; to abandon equally what we see and what we possess, our power, our knowledge, and our affections; so that the soul in regard to any action originating in itself, is without life, without action, and without power, and receives its life, its action, and its power from God alone." Were the early Christians called upon to sunder the tenderest ties of affection, if necessary, to their own spiritual good, and the advancement of Christ's cause? The same is true of ourselves. Is the Saviour less worthy of *our* highest love? May any earthly attachment be allowed to usurp the place of that supreme attachment due to him?

Pursuing the path of duty, it often becomes necessary, in order to the highest good, to sacrifice social, parental, and filial affection. As of old, one's foes are sometimes those of his own household. Obedience to Christ sets at variance "a man against his father, and the daughter against her mother, and the daughter-in-law against her mother-in-law." In other cases it becomes necessary that the most endeared society and companionship of mutual friends be interrupted; perhaps a missionary parent being called to tear himself from his own children, born in heathen lands, but now, of necessity, placed beyond their corrupting influences, or a sister or brother responding to the divine call, and forsaking father and brother to go far hence to the Gentiles, or toil in some distant and inaccessible portion of the Lord's vineyard. But, trying as is the loss of esteemed friendship, and keen as is the anguish attending the separation of those long united, it must be endured; for unless the heart cling with more ardent feelings and a firmer grasp to Jesus Christ, than to parents or children, or sisters or brothers, how can we suppose ourselves, according to Christ's representations, to be his disciples?

And so of houses and lands, and gold and silver, the material treasures of earth. Why should our Saviour's language concerning the duty of forsaking all these, for his sake and the gospel's, be considered as exclusively, or even especially, applicable to Christians of primitive times? Is not the love of money, in our day, just as truly "the root of all evil?" Is it not even more liable to come into competition with the supreme love of Christ? Can *we* "love the world, and the things that are in the world," and yet have within us the "love of the Father?" Can we cleave to our property, and hug our possessions, when Christ is calling us to relinquish them for the good of his cause, and still be his disciples? Let us not deceive ourselves. Let us rest assured that it is as true now as formerly, that he that is not ready, at Christ's requirement, to forsake "*all that he hath*," cannot be his disciple.

Thus much has seemed necessary to the proper development of the divine law of self-denial; considered in reference to its uses, the method and spirit of its exercise, its partial illustration in the remotest periods of the world, its complete development in the example of Christ and his immediate followers, and in his own positive instructions, and, finally, in its universal applicability.

And this examination has rendered obvious a most important conclusion; which is, that *self-denial is the great law of the Christian religion.* It is nothing less than an actual condition of discipleship. When we are first found of Christ, we are in love of self and the world. That love is supreme.

But the whole tendency of Christianity is in the contrary direction. Christ must be exalted, and become "all in all." Self must be abased, and the Saviour enthroned in the soul. There is, there can be *no* true conversion where the dominion of selfishness is not broken. And there can be no *progress* in religion without it. An ingenious writer remarks that "there is just as much religion as there is self-denial." "Our religion," says Dr. Griffin, "is exactly in proportion as we are borne away by the love of God and his creatures from self, and stand ready, from that heavenly principle, to sacrifice personal ease, comfort, and property, to advance the kingdom of righteousness."

There are no two things under heaven more antagonistic, than are self-indulgence and growth in grace. Some trees bear fruit most plentifully when the branches are hung with weights; and so God's children "bear much fruit" when they daily, hourly, bear the cross. This was the experience of Henry Martyn. "A despicable indulgence," says he, "gave me such a view of my character that on my knees I resolved to live a life of greater self-denial. The love and vigor of my mind rose rapidly, and all those duties from which I usually shrank, seemed recreaations." And the testimony of this devoted servant of Christ is confirmed by the experience of every true Christian.

We come now to the inquiry, *Is there a just measure of this self-denial for Christ among the Christians of the present day?* Let the general *reluctance of professedly pious parents, to give up their sons as missionaries to the heathen*, testify.

A missionary once remarked, that many parents were quite ready to consecrate their children to this service before they were converted. "O if the Saviour would only convert my child, I would readily yield him to go to any part of the world, and to perform any service for which he might be fitted." But that when the child becomes converted, the parents cling to him, and dissuade him from devoting himself to the service, if he is drawn toward it. The testimony is too true.

It is stated that, of twenty or more young men in a theological institution, who were at the same time agitating the question of their duty to become missionaries, all but two were discouraged by their parents, and these two were the sons of widows. Does this look like the self-denial of primitive times?

Again; let the *treasuries of our benevolent societies* testify upon the question proposed. That self-denial in giving of their substance for the furtherance of Christ's cause, is not practised among Christians, to any considerable extent, would seem too obvious to require proof. It is true that within a half century, it has become quite customary for the members of the churches to contribute for the promotion of benevolent enterprises, and that in some instances the wealthy give largely.

But this does not affect the question before us. What *is* self-denial? Is it, as one has asked, to give liberally of our income, yet withholding for ourselves the whole of the vested wealth from which it is derived? Is it to make large donations to the destitute and miserable, retaining enough to live according to the fashion of this world, in luxury and splendor? It is something far removed from all this. To decide the question of self-denial, let it be asked, not "what have you given?" but "*what have you kept?*" You plead that you have given. Admit it, but have you not also *withheld?* And if you have withheld so as to admit of a life of luxurious extravagance, where is your self-denial? "I contribute as much as I conveniently can," is an expression sometimes heard; and it defines the popular standard of giving. And yet how strange an expression to be found in a Christian's lips! "As much as I *conveniently* can contribute!" As if *convenience* were the arbitrator to which one might refer the amount of his charity! Then if your style of living is only sufficiently extravagant, you will have nothing to give, for it will swallow up your entire income! Upon this principle the most wealthy will oftentimes have the least to bestow. Suppose that Christ had listened to the dictates of *convenience*, — and the good men and true of ages past, the benefactors of their race, — what had been the present stage of human progress? Nay, Christian, what had been your prospects for eternity?

And suppose, again, that the early disciples had possessed as little of the liberal, self-sacrificing spirit as is now generally possessed. Suppose that *our* type of character, as regards self-denial, had been *theirs?* With their deep poverty, and serious obstacles to rapid communication, and their limited numbers, how narrow a circle would have bounded their influence, and how small a space would have sufficed to record the history of their achievements! It is a most humiliating reflection that the type of our piety in this respect, is so nearly the reverse of the primitive model, that instances of true, heroic self-denial, are the rare *exceptions* of a general fact. Men who practise it, are looked upon almost with astonishment, at least with admiration; and their example is thus conspicuous, only because it differs so widely from that of others. Would it have been thus in the time of the apostles?

It is to be feared that economizing, even, for the purpose of increasing benevolent expenditures, is a thing of comparatively infrequent occurrence. Saving by economy is indeed common; but for what purpose? Is it often done *for Christ*, with the single object of being able to contribute toward the advancement of his cause in the earth? And surely, though it is not within the province of any one to prescribe for others rules of retrenchment, and show precisely how much or how little they must give, or may retain, yet, all will admit, that *the least* that can be required of any individual is, that he *save by economy* in order to swell the rills of his benevolence.

But if such examples are infrequent, much more so are examples of *personal sacrifice for Christ.* We know what it is to make sacrifices for others, — what sacrifices, for instance, will parents make for their children! If a son is lost, or imprisoned, in some distant country, or cast upon some lonely island, how ready to provide, at any expense and sacrifice, the means of his deliverance! Or if sick and threatened with speedy death, money is not thought of, personal comfort is not taken into the account, nor health, nor, in some cases, life itself, if the loved one may but recover.

And there are *some* instances of sacrificing for the sake of Christ. A missionary mother, as she kneeled upon the sand by the sea-shore, after placing on board ship her darling offspring, now separated forever from her fond embrace, exclaimed, as she looked toward heaven, "O JESUS, I DO THIS FOR THEE!"

Other examples of noble self-immolation are known and recorded; and others still are unknown of men, but observed and remembered of God. But *how few* Christians voluntarily subject themselves to real sacrifices of any kind, that by this means God may be glorified, and men saved from the wrath which is to come! "We ought," says the Apostle John, "*to lay down our lives for the breth-*

ren." But, alas! how few are ready to lay down even their *personal ease* and *comfort!* How few will give until they *feel it*, absolutely denying and sacrificing *self* for Christ!

Once more, let evidence be gathered from the general style of living, as to the measure of self-denial now prevalent. We are speaking of *Christians;* and one of the divine commands addressed to them is, "*Be not conformed to this world.*" As to the exact demands of this law, in its varied applications, many doubts and differences of opinion will naturally exist. But one thing is certain: it contemplates a difference between Christians and other men. They are "*a peculiar people;*" and it is expected of them that their feelings, and motives, and actions will be unlike those of others. They are not to be governed by the laws, and opinions, and practices of this world. Men of the world have *their* laws, — laws of fashion, ambition, honor. Parents make laws for their families; and kings and statesmen for their country; and those for whose control and welfare they are made, are expected to submit to them. They are not to conform to the laws of *other* families and countries; they are not called upon to obey them; for they belong to different communities, and owe allegiance to different authorities.

So of Christians. They are a community by themselves. They are different from other men, among whom they are to shine as lights in the world. They acknowledge a different king, even Jesus Christ. They have placed themselves under his authority, have pledged fidelity to him, and promised to be governed by his laws, and by his alone. They are in the world, and must, of necessity, be in many things like the men of the world. But they are not to regulate their opinions and conduct by those of worldly men; they are not to seek their approbation or applause, or dread and shrink from their disapprobation, if incurred in well-doing; they are not to pursue their pleasures, and follies, and amusements, and be influenced by their motives and manner of life. In a word, they are to conduct themselves as pilgrims and strangers upon the earth, whose citizenship is in heaven; as a people distinct from other men, living for a time in the world, but nevertheless living above it.

Such is the acknowledged import of the precept forbidding our conformity to this world, and of many other Scriptures of a similar nature. But if some celestial being were to visit our earth, and mingle in our affairs, and pass through our houses, would he be led to infer the existence of any such broad distinction as that which has been described? Should he enter one of our large cities, and behold the magnificent houses, "grand equipages," and "splendid entertainments," and all the pomp and vanities of "high life," which may be seen in these days in many *Christian* families, what would be his surprise on being informed, that among those who roll in such voluptuousness, and perhaps are striving to be foremost in the gay procession, are the professed followers of the *humble, self-denying Jesus!* And would it be less surprising that in the village and country parish, the customs of "the city" were "all the rage;" and that everywhere, throughout the length and breadth of the land, the rich and the poor were gathering around the car of *fashion*, that "Juggernaut of Christian lands," eager to do homage?

The simple truth is, the world has been suffered to give laws to the church; whereas the church should have given laws to the world. And the worst of all is, there is a general concurrence in this usurpation. "It is *customary*," is the universal plea. "We shall be deemed *singular*, if we do not thus or so." This is enough to pacify the conscience, and thus the tide of extravagance flows on, few raising the question of good old Bunyan, "Why follow the apish fashions of the world? Hath the God of wisdom set them on foot among us? or is it because the devil and wicked men, the inventors of these vain toys, have outwitted the law of God?"

Imitating the example of those by whom they are surrounded, Christians have generally fallen into a luxurious, self-indulgent style of living. And the evil is daily increasing. The merchant prince, "who enjoyed his domestic establishment at an expense of $2,000 or $3,000 a year, *endures* one, now, which demands five or ten times that sum; and the wife, who graced a $20 or $50 shawl, disgraces herself and her profession with one costing from $500 to $1,000." It were well if this foolish rage for show were limited to particular localities. Its prevalence accounts, to a great extent, for the small amount bestowed in charity. In most cases it requires nearly the whole income to support the favorite style of living; certainly "to lay by something for a time of need."

Hence, as one has it, "men are draught-horses of mammon. Women are slaves. Life, falsely organized, grinds God's children between its upper and nether mill-stone."* They are incapacitated for any thing beyond the most limited benevolence, and even for the enjoyment of a contented, peaceful life, amid the good things which they *might* enjoy, by the pressure of a desire "to keep up appearances," and not fall behind some neighbor or acquaintance, whom they are secretly attempting to rival.

Beyond all question, the various channels of unnecessary expenditure are, to-day, draining from the professedly religious families of our land, a sum of money, which, if rightly appropriated, would prove adequate to the broadest scale of Christian benevolence. Let these be cut off, and there would be found an abundance, both for personal comfort and culture, and for the cause of Christ. No careful observer of society as now organized, can doubt the truth of the remark, that where avarice, or hoarding, has slain its thousands, a lavish profusion has slain its tens of thousands: and where the former robs the cause of God of a mite, the latter robs it of a million.

A return, therefore, of the self-sacrificing spirit of the primitive Christians, is a grand necessity of the times. Dr. Neander, in his History of the Christian Religion during the First Three Centuries, says, with reference to the struggle which the early Christians were obliged to maintain against a conformity to the customs of society: "This struggle might indeed have been partially avoided, had the early church, like the churches of later days, been inclined to humor the world, had they at least accommodated

---

* Dr. George B. Cheever.

themselves to the prevailing manners, even when opposed to Christianity, merely to obtain more followers. But the first Christians were far more inclined to a haughty abomination of every thing heathen, and even of that which had merely *an apparent* connection with paganism, than to any thing like a lax accommodation."

It is precisely this spirit that is now required. Instead of indulging in a "lax accommodation" to "humor the world," we need to '*come out of the world and be separate.*' Is Christ's kingdom just like other kingdoms? Are his followers just like other men? Can it be that they are so to live as to render it difficult to distinguish them from the impenitent multitude by whom they are surrounded? Can it be that the masses of men in Christian lands, who are without God in the world, are so closely conformed, in their lives, to the divine standard, that it is safe for Christians to take their pattern from them?

Far otherwise. It is still true, that while "we are of God," "the whole world lieth in wickedness." Men of the world are not the friends of Christ. They still are the enemies of the cross; and such as 'will live godly shall still suffer persecution.'

Christian countries are, in an important sense, *unchristian.* The prevailing influence is not that of the gospel. And the followers of Jesus are in danger of being contaminated by that influence, and losing "*the simplicity that is in Christ.*" To resist it, requires moral courage. As large a measure of self-denial is requisite, on our part, to withstand the tide of worldly influence, as was requisite on the part of the early Christians. The martyr-spirit is still essen tial to a life of eminent godliness. And this spirit waits a resurrection. It shall yet be revived. The time is coming when men shall act less from impulse and convenience in matters of religion, and more from *principle;* when they shall more attentively study the divine word, inquiring within themselves, "*what sort of a person, in thought and in feeling and in action, was my* SAVIOUR?" and esteeming it their highest honor to be like unto him in all things.

"Our blessed Lord," says an early Christian writer, "ate his food from a common dish. He sat upon the ground, and washed his disciples' feet without a silver basin. Nay, he quenched his thirst from the earthen pitcher of a poor Samaritan woman. And are we better than he? Will not a table contain our food, unless its legs be ivory? Certain it is, that a lamp made by a potter will give light as well as if it were the work of a silversmith."

The time is coming when Christians shall answer to the device of an ancient medal, now adopted by a modern missionary association, representing a bullock standing between a plough and an altar, with the inscription, "*Ready for either.*" Ready to drag and swelter in the field of service, or bleed on the altar of sacrifice.

The time is coming when one may easily discern between the righteous and the wicked; when the saints of the Most High shall be like unto their brethren of former times, of whom one of their own number says, "They inhabit their native land, but only as sojourners. They take a part in all things as citizens, but endure all things as foreigners; every foreign country is to them a native land, and every native country a foreign land. . . . They live in the flesh, but not after the flesh. They pass their time on earth, but their citizenship is in heaven. They obey the existing laws, but in their lives they transcend all laws. They love all and are persecuted by all. They live unknown and are condemned to death. They are slain, and behold they live." *

The time is coming when men will look back upon what is called the *Christian activity* of this age, with even greater surprise than we contemplate the inactivity of those who have preceded us; when our brightest illustrations of self-denial for Christ, shall become so common as to attract no special attention; and those who exhibit, in this respect, no more of the spirit of Christ than is now exhibited by the mass of professors, will be hardly acknowledged as worthy of the Christian name.

Then shall Zion have put on her strength, and naught shall resist her progress. Then, by an argument of irresistible power, shall men be persuaded of the reality of our holy religion; and, dispossessed of self, " God, even our God, shall bless us; God shall bless us, and all the ends of the earth shall fear him."

Nor are we left in ignorance as to the means and motives by which an increase of this spirit is to be secured. They are furnished in the *cross of Christ.* The great actuating principle in evangelical piety is *love.* Other motives to holy obedience there are,

---

* Epistle to Diognetus. See this beautiful fragment of early Christian literature entire in Dr. Turnbull's " *Christ in History, or the Central Power among Men.*"

but, compared with this, they hold a rank of minor importance. "*The love of Christ constraineth us.*" This is the hidden mainspring that sets in motion every part of our being.

> ''T is love that makes our cheerful feet
> In swift obedience move.'

Love prompts to entire devotion. "Every drop of my blood thanks you," cried a condemned criminal, as he cast himself at the feet of Dr. Doddridge, who had procured his pardon, "for you have had mercy upon every drop of it. Wherever you go, *I will be yours.*" Love inspires the desire to please. We are slow to grieve a bosom friend. Said our Saviour, "If a man *love* me he *will keep* my words." It cannot be otherwise. And hence the strong language of some of the early Christians, on whose hearts the pure flame of love burned so brightly. "It seems to me," said one, "much more bitter to offend Christ, than to be tormented in hell." Another declares, "I say the truth, if on one hand I saw the pains of hell, and on the other the horror of sinning against the love of Jesus, and I must be plunged in one, I would choose the pains of hell,—I could never sin against this love." We, too, could adopt such language, if, like them we were so full of love divine, as to be 'beside ourselves unto God.'

Love leads to ready sacrifices. From the force of this principle, the mother disregards her own comfort for the babe of her bosom; the father or husband lavishes his hard earnings upon a companion, or children; and the patriot sacrifices himself for the good of his country. "What a pity," cried the

Roman, "that we have but one life for our country!" Christ's yoke is easy, and his burden is light, when we are borne upward and onward by the transporting power of love.

Now this grace, like all others, grows by exercise. And where else is it called into exercise, as at the cross of Christ? *How much* the Saviour loved us, is best seen in what he has done and suffered for us. In like manner our love to him is best proved by doing his will and bearing his cross. At his cross must we linger, if we would awaken all that is tender in affection, and self-sacrificing in devotion. On Calvary is found "a demonstration to convince the mind, and a talisman to kindle the heart." How *can* we fail to love Christ, and strengthen the principle of entire self-devotement, if we study our obligations at the foot of the cross?

Under the inspiration of the affecting scenes that cluster around that sacred spot, self-denial becomes a *pleasure*. It is a positive *relief* to suffer. We rejoice that we are counted *worthy* of it, and are dissatisfied with ourselves if not suffering. We cannot, we *will* not be contented to offer to him that which costs us nothing; but 'gratitude will cast all her living into the treasury of the Lord, and Love will pour her most "precious ointment" upon the Saviour's dying head; the one, feeling that her *all* is too little, and the other, that her most costly tribute is too poor to express the fervor of her affection, and the entireness of her devotion.'

And, finally, as to *yourself*, dear reader, what is the measure of *your* self-denial? You know the grace of our Lord Jesus Christ; how that, though he was rich, yet for our sakes he became poor, that we through his poverty might be made rich. *How rich was he!* rich in honor, and glory, and dominion, and bliss, and power! And *how poor* did he become for our sakes! What poverty marked his birth and his entire history! And added to this, what crushing sorrows, what overwhelming sufferings, has he endured for you! And what returns have you rendered? *How much have* YOU *suffered for* HIM*?* Can you suffer *too much?* Is there any sacrifice too costly to present, as a feeble expression of your grateful emotions?

O no! As you behold that suffering Saviour, you cannot but count your best gifts as mean and nothing worth; and from your heart exclaim,

"Were the whole realm of nature mine,
  That were a present *far too small:*
Love so amazing, so divine,
  Demands my *soul*, my *life*, my ALL!"

CHAPTER V.

THE WANT OF A SCRIPTURAL FAITH, A GRAND DEFECT IN THE PREVAILING TYPE OF PIETY.

Faith defined. — Scriptural Examples. — Sublime Results. — Brings to view Eternal Things. — Secures Sanctification. — Imparts Activity and Strength. — Enables us to overcome the World. — A Scriptural Faith not prevalent. — Skepticism in the Church. — As to Prayer and Missions, and other Departments of Christian Duty. — A Faith such as is requisite, entirely practicable. — Its Possession a cardinal Necessity of any Age. — Spiritual Enemies the same. — World not modified in favor of the Church, but the Church in favor of the World. — Faith of Martyr Age still demanded. — Efforts to be made for its Attainment. — May be increased. — How effected. — Glorious Results of Return of Primitive Faith. — The Grand Remedy of all existing Defects.

How lucid the exposition of faith as given in that "Roll-call of the Dead," — the eleventh chapter of the Epistle to the Hebrews! "Now faith is the substance of things hoped for, the evidence of things not seen." It is the "*substance*," — that which is placed under, the ground, the basis, the foundation; and hence the *firm confidence*, answering to the *actual existence* — "of things hoped for." Or, to take the other branch of the definition, it is the "*evidence* of things not seen;" the *evincing* or *bringing to light*, and hence the *proof* of them; being equivalent to, or supplying the place of, actual demonstration. As if it had been said, We do not *see* the objects of the future world, — God, angels, the redeemed, the crowns of righteousness, the robes of glory, — but to him who has *faith* they are not unreal and imaginary, but *positive realities;* this faith answering for their very *substance*, presenting them in bold relief, and influencing its possessor just as if he saw them with his natural eyes.

"It is the very nature of faith to give an uncontrollable efficacy to objects *invisible* and *distant.* All must allow that the things which God has revealed would have a mighty influence upon us, if they were actually *visible* and *present.* To faith they *are* visible. To faith they are *present* too. Faith removes the distance, and makes them present realities. So that things which are not seen, and things which are to take place thousands of ages hence, excite the same emotions, and have the same practical influence, as though they were actually visible, and actually present. They are equally interesting to us, as if they were present; for they *will* be present; and we shall experience them and feel them, when happiness will be as dear to us, and misery as dreadful, as they are now. They deserve our regard, therefore, just as though they were present. So that, if the infinite excellences of God, and the employments and pleasures of heaven are sufficient to move the hearts and govern the actions of saints and angels who are now there, they are sufficient to move and govern *us.* If the transactions of the judgment-day, if the glorious appearing of the Lord from heaven, the assembling of the universe before him, the disclosure of the secrets of all hearts, the final sentence, the blessedness of the righteous, and the horror and despair of the wicked, will be sufficient to arrest the attention, and touch the feelings, and move all the active powers of those who will be present on that momentous occasion; they are sufficient to arrest our attention, to touch our feelings, and move all our powers of action *now*. And just so far as we have faith, they will do it. Men generally look at things which are seen. Sensible objects govern their affections, and limit the sphere of their observation. But faith shifts the scene. As to the grand, governing objects of the human mind, and the motives to action, it puts them in a new world. It spreads a shroud over the things of time and sense, and opens to view things unseen and eternal." *

Having defined faith, the writer gives examples of its wonderworking power. We are told how it wrought in Abel, and Enoch, and Noah; in Abraham, and Isaac, and Jacob, and Joseph, and Moses. Beyond these, others are mentioned; who, through faith, subdued kingdoms, wrought righteousness, obtained promises, stopped the mouths of lions, quenched the violence of fire, escaped the edge of the sword, out of weakness were made strong, waxed valiant in fight, and turned to flight the armies of aliens. And others still are declared to have been tortured, and tried, and mocked, and scourged, and stoned, and sawn asunder, and slain; or wandered about destitute, afflicted, and tormented, in the dens and caves of the earth, and yet to have obtained through faith a good report. 'What these

---

* See Tract No. 13, of the Cong. Board Series.

servants of God did and suffered was by faith. Objects of the future and invisible world, seemed as present realities, and in their esteem contained a blessedness so great and precious, that it roused all their desires and all their efforts; and in pursuit of it hardships and sufferings become light, and the most painful enterprises easy and pleasant. Such was the power of faith.' Placing before us these and other scriptural representations of this heavenly grace, its nature is easily perceived.

Faith is belief in things beyond our observation. It is, in particular, *confidence in God*, — a firm, cordial belief in the *existence* of the Most High, and in his *veracity*, — a full and affectionate persuasion of the *certainty* of what God has declared, and simply because he has declared it. It is not reasoning, but believing; not a process of demonstration, but *naked trust. The Lord hath spoken*, is enough. This cuts short all debate, and hushes to silence every objection. The word of the Lord is infallible, and so it becomes a foundation for the most certain truths.

The Scriptures have much to say upon faith. No attentive reader of the Bible can have failed to observe the frequency with which it is made the subject of remark. And with reason: for behold its sublime and beneficent results.

Faith *brings to view eternal things*. The objects of religion are invisible, inaudible, impalpable. No man hath seen God at any time; nor may we perceive with mortal eyes, the spirits of just men made perfect, nor heaven, nor hell. But faith reveals them to our view.

"It pierces through the veil of sense,
And dwells in heavenly light."

'And therefore the apostle says of himself and his brethren, "We walk by faith, not by sight," as much as to say, faith is the essential principle, or motive power of the Christian life. "*We walk*,—*not by sight*," that is, we are not influenced in our conduct by a regard to the things which are seen. But *we walk by faith*, in things unseen. And how are those unseen spiritual and eternal objects made known, so that the Christian is influenced by them in all his walk and conversation, but by faith? And hence Peter speaks of faith as purifying the heart and overcoming the world. It is by presenting to the mind those unseen, spiritual, and eternal objects, as though they were present, and thus faith has a controlling influence over the affections and the life.'

Faith *insures happiness* to the child of God. We have "joy and peace *in believing*." The gospel is glad tidings to the soul that has faith to credit them. It assures the child of God that Jesus liveth to make intercession for him, that every necessity shall be supplied, that every dark stain of sin shall be cleansed away in the blood of Christ, and that there awaits him in heaven, an inheritance that is "incorruptible, undefiled, and that fadeth not away."

Faith *secures our sanctification*. The believing soul accepts the word of God,—the grand instrumentality in the work of sanctification,—*as* the word of God. It comes to him with authority. It is clothed with power. He trembles before its awful sanctions, and rejoices in view of its blessed assurances. And by each class of truths is he led to flee from sin, and follow after holiness. How *can* he transgress if he credit what is written? The presence of God forbids it. His majesty makes him afraid. His holiness shames him to contrition and confession; and his love constrains him to holy obedience. The cross overpowers him. He *believes* that his Saviour hung there. He *feels* that he died for him on the tree, to save him from the curse of sin. How *can* he live any longer in sin? How can he crucify afresh his *best friend*, and put him to an open shame.

> "O the sweet wonders of that cross
> Where God the Saviour loved and died!"

Can he stand beside that cross, and *see*, as he does see, by faith, the bleeding, dying Lamb of God,—bleeding and dying for *him*,—and *commit sin?* Impossible. He must turn away, first, from that sight. He must cease, in some sense, to *believe*, before he can willingly transgress.

Moreover, faith promotes the sanctification of the soul by holding it in intimate union and communion with Christ. The believer, by faith, is kept in vital connection with the Saviour; whence he derives spiritual life, as the branch draws nourishment from the vine. I am crucified with Christ: nevertheless I live: yet not I, but Christ liveth in me: and the life which I now live in the flesh I live by the faith of the Son of God, who loved me, and gave himself for me. A living member of that body of which Christ is the Head, the spirit of Christ enters into him, and pervades every fibre of his whole being. The vital influence from his Lord warms and invigorates his heart. 'Because Christ lives, he lives also;' and because Christ 'was dead unto sin,' he 'dies daily unto sin.' Thus *by faith* does he live upon the Son of God, and become more and more conformed to his image.

It may be added, that the experience of every Christian is in striking harmony with these representations. When faith is wanting or feeble, every virtue declines: when it is strong, every Christian grace is vigorous and active.

The testimony of Richard Baxter is here much in point. Referring to a certain temptation to unbelief, he says, " From this assault I was forced to take notice, that our belief of the truth of the word of God and of the life to come, *is the spring of all grace;* and with which it rises or falls, flourishes or decays, is actuated or stands still; and that there is more of this secret *unbelief* at the bottom, than most of us are aware of; and that our love of the world, our boldness in sin, our neglect of duty, are caused hence. I easily observed in myself, that, if at any time, Satan, more than at other times, weakened my belief of the Scripture and of the life to come, my zeal in every religious duty abated with it, and I grew more indifferent in religion than before. But when FAITH REVIVED, then none of the parts or concerns of religion seemed small; and then man seemed nothing, and the world a shadow, and God was all."

Faith imparts *Christian courage.* It nerves one to suffer and endure for the sake of Christ. Heaven is opened to the vision of one who truly believes; and forgetting the trials of this present time in view of the glorious prospect, he exclaims, " None of these things move me, neither count I my life dear unto myself, so that I might finish my course with joy." The deity is to him a *present God;* he feels the girdings of divine power, and 'what time he is afraid, he trusts in him.'

Hence the fortitude of a Nehemiah, whose language was, "Should such a man as I flee?" — of a Paul, who was ready to die even for his religion, — of a Polycarp, who did die for it, and who could say, when urged to blaspheme Christ on pain of death, "Eighty and six years have I served Christ, and he has never done me an injury; how can I blaspheme my King and my Saviour?" and on being threatened with burning alive, declared, "I fear not the fire that burns for a moment; thou knowest not that which burns forever and ever!" — of a Chrysostom, who, in reply to the threats sent to him from the hand of supreme authority, said, "Go, tell Eudoxia that I fear nothing but sin!" — and of a Luther, who would go up to the Diet at Worms, 'if there were as many devils there as tiles upon the roofs of the houses.' Thus does faith prepare the soldier of the cross to meet the divine requirement, "Be thou very courageous."

Faith *imparts activity and strength.* In ordinary instances, to say the least, there is an exact proportion between our strength of belief, and our strength of purpose. A strong faith makes a strong will. A feeble purpose is the offspring of a feeble faith. And so of action. Confidence induces perseverance and energy. Unbelief benumbs the powers.

> "—— Our doubts are traitors,
> And make us lose the good we oft might win,
> By fearing to attempt."

Faith, in the broad acceptation of *belief*, underlies all great actions. Confidence is at the same time the condition and the pledge of success. Milton had a foreshadowing of his sublime production, long before it was matured in his mind. Many years before he commenced his task, he declared his intention of writing some great poem for posterity which "the world would not willingly let die." Illustrations to almost any extent, might be adduced showing this power of assurance in the production of sublime results.

If, in the things of this world, a deep persuasion of final success leads to noble achievements, if under the influence of this persuasion, men will brook no denials, and cower before no difficulties, — how much more intrepid and energetic might he be expected to be, who is possessed of that *spiritual* energy, that wonderworking faith which is the gift of God! "The firmest thing in this lower world," says Leighton, "is a believing soul." And with reason; for it has hold upon divine power; it is allied to the Almighty; the impotence of the creature is linked to the omnipotence of Jehovah. "All things are possible to him that believeth."

> "Faith, mighty faith, the promise sees,
> And looks to that alone;
> Laughs at impossibilities
> And cries, it shall be done."

Full of faith, the believer is in actual experience of the presence, at his side, of him who said, "Lo, I am with you alway, even unto the end of the world." He sees him near at hand, and not afar off. He hears his words of sweet assurance; and, knowing that all power is given unto Christ, it is to him as though that power were in himself.

The connection between confidence in God, and dauntless, energetic activity in his service, is apparent from the method which our Lord adopted, fully to qualify his followers for their trials and labors. How intent was he upon strengthening their faith! Anxious to know the cause of their inability to expel a demon, they are told that it was because of their *unbelief.* Amazed that a fig-tree should so soon wither under the frown of their Master, they are taught that, 'if they have faith and doubt not,' at their word trees should be plucked up, and mountains should be carried into the midst of the sea. And, in saying to them, as oft in substance he did, "According to your faith be it unto you," "If ye abide in me, and my words abide in you, ye shall ask what ye will, and it shall be done unto you," what less was it than saying, '*the amount of your faith shall be the measure of your success?*'*

* "Of course this, like all other promises and precepts of the gospel, must be taken with such limitations as are necessarily involved in the nature of the case. The prayer must be real prayer, the faith must be genuine and wellgrounded faith, and the objects must be proper objects of desire; or, as the Apostle John defines them, "things according to the will of God." For this is only saying, that the faith must be such faith as the disciples of Christ might be expected to exercise, the prayer such prayer as they would be likely to offer, and the objects such objects as they would naturally and reasonably desire, *under the divine teachings of his Word and Spirit.* Without such limitations the promise was not fulfilled to the very chief of the apostles. With these necessary and obvious limitations, it was literally

And was not this *true* of the immediate followers of Christ? Did they not *believe* beyond a peradventure, what the Lord had spoken? Were they not mighty in deed *because* they were "mighty in faith;" even as is related of Barnabas, that he was 'full of faith,' and that 'much people was added unto the Lord?' Is it not also true of the successful workers in our day? Is not the remarkable success of many of our missionaries ascribable to the large measure of their faith? Cut off from human sympathies and resources, — impressed with a sense of their own impotence in so vast an undertaking, they learn to fall back upon the strong arm of God. Shut up to an unwavering reliance upon the simple promise and pledge of the Most High, this promise and pledge becomes, as by necessity, their only support, and in their weakness God perfects his strength.

---

and gloriously fulfilled to the entire body of the primitive disciples. And in their undoubting reliance on this promise, in their habitual use of this Divine weapon, lay the secret of their strength, and the certainty of their triumph.

"With the same limitations, the promise is just as real, just as literal, just as reliable, and just as full of truth and power now, as it ever was. All things whatsoever that we ask in real prayer, and genuine, wellgrounded faith, and *according to the will of God*, we shall receive. The time may be delayed, the manner may be unexpected, but sooner or later, in some form or other, the answer to believing prayer is sure to come, — to come in God's own best time and way.

"We cannot talk with God face to face like Abraham, nor open and shut the heavens like Elijah, nor heal the sick and raise the dead like Peter and John and Paul, but our importunate intercessions, — our oft-repeated supplications, may bring down copious showers of spiritual blessings upon the waste places of our Zion." — Prayer for Colleges, by Professor Tyler.

Adoniram Judson, during a visit to the United States, was asked by a friend, "Do you think the prospects bright for the speedy conversion of the heathen?" "As bright," was his prompt reply, "as the promises of God." And what one has said of him, is doubtless applicable to many a missionary of the cross. His faith seemed "to place him in direct communication with God. It never appeared to him possible, for a moment, that God could fail to do *precisely as he had said;* and he therefore relied on the divine assurance with a confidence that excluded all wavering. He believed that Burmah was to be converted to Christ, just as much as he believed that Burmah existed. He believed that he had been sent there to preach the gospel, and he as much believed that the Holy Ghost would make his labors, in some way, or at some time, the means of the salvation of the nation, as he believed that there was a Holy Ghost. In prayer he asked not as a duty, nor even as a pleasure, but he asked that he might receive. He acted on the assurance that his heavenly Father delighted to bestow upon him whatever was for his best good. It was a common thing for him to ask until he received in his own consciousness an assurance that his requests would be granted."* Is

* Wayland's Memoir of Dr. Judson, Vol. II. pp. 380, 381.

When Samuel J. Mills was about to leave home to attend school, his mother, anxious for her son, took this opportunity to inquire into the state of his mind. In a season of revival young Mills had been deeply exercised with a sense of his own sinfulness. He had felt great hostility to the sovereignty of God in showing mercy to those around him, while he himself was left to obduracy and unbelief, and he frankly disclosed these feelings to it surprising that men of *such* faith should toil on amidst all possible discouragements, and that God should constitute them his prime agents, in subduing unto himself a revolted race?

And, finally, as regards the results of faith, it enables us *to overcome the world.* "THIS IS THE VICTORY THAT OVERCOMETH THE WORLD, EVEN OUR FAITH." That is, faith is the *source*, or *means* of the victory which we achieve over the world. Its evil examples,

---

his mother, and soon took his leave for the winter. His farewell to his mother under these circumstances drove her to her knees, to plead for her poor son. And God was pleased to show her that all her help was in him, and to enable her to feel that to him could her heart turn as her only God in covenant. She did not leave her closet till she found the full relief she sought, and till her mind was confidently assured that God would remember mercy for her child! And on that very morning it pleased the Holy Spirit, as she afterwards ascertained, to knock off the chains from this unhappy prisoner, and introduce him into the liberty of the sons of God. He had not gone far after thus leaving his mother, before he had such a view of the perfections of God, that he wondered he had never seen their beauty and glory before. He had lost all his opposition to the divine sovereignty, and such were his views of this adorable perfection that he could not refrain from exclaiming, "O glorious sovereignty! O glorious sovereignty!" There was a wonderful change. The scene was altogether new. Every thing was gilded with light and glory, and as he gazed at the splendor and majesty of the divine character, he would still exclaim, "O glorious sovereignty!" Such was the answer to this mother's prayer. And this is one of the thousand cases to illustrate that there is such a thing as special faith in prayer. It was such to this dear saint when she went to plead for her poor son. She deeply felt his sorrows and her own, and with earnest importunity she plead, and her prayer prevailed with God.— See Life of Samuel J. Mills, by Dr. Spring.

— its false principles, — and false promises, and its persecutions, — every thing in the world that is opposed to the religion of the gospel, — as we are here taught, we overcome by faith. The victory spoken of, is "the subordination in the state of our mind, of the creature to the Creator; of earth to heaven; of temporal blessings to spiritual ones; of time to eternity. It is the formation of an unearthly, spiritual, divine, heavenly character." This victory is gained by means of *faith;* which is the line of communication between heaven and earth, along which travels down from God's throne to the human heart, that principle which fills it with a strange and mighty energy.

And *how* does faith operate, in securing to us this victory? By putting us into communication with Christ, as just intimated. Christ himself has already achieved this victory. He says, "Be of good cheer; I have overcome the world." He excites in the bosom of the disciple no false hope of ease and undisturbed tranquillity; but, on the contrary, assures him that 'in the world he shall have tribulation.' "It is enough that the disciple be as his Master." Yet, if he is left to no uncertainty as to his trial, neither is he as to his success. However sharp the struggle, by faith the Christian soldier sees the Captain of our salvation beckoning to him from the skies, and reaching out to view the glorious prize; while above the din of the conflict is heard the animating voice, "*I have overcome the world!*" "I have given you the example, and secured for you the victory!" "*Be thou faithful unto death, and I will give thee a crown of life!*" By this means is the child of God strengthened with might in the inner man. Practically, the Saviour is about him and within him. It is not so much himself, weak as he is, that maintains the contest, as Christ that liveth in him, — not so much his weakness as the Redeemer's almightiness.

Thus does faith, in acting as the medium of communication between Christ and the believer, enable him to overcome the world. It tends to this result, also, by leading us to suppress unholy desires, and put away the remains of corruption within. But for our inward depravity, outward temptation would be powerless. Now faith, by attaching itself to the divine promises of assistance in struggling for victory over our corrupt natures, and by inducing that love which leads us to fear lest we offend God by indulging the sordid propensities, tends to the removal from within us of whatsoever is evil, and the development of whatsoever is good. The same is true of Satan's "fiery darts," which are, oftentimes, nothing less than some mighty temptation of the world, which the adversary seizes upon for our destruction. Hence faith is termed a "shield" by which we "quench" those darts; and few men have been better qualified to testify of its efficacy, from personal experience, than was one who has said, "None knows save he that feels it, how fiery hot the darts of Satan are; and how, when darted, they kindle upon the flesh and unbelief; neither can any know the power and worth of *faith* to quench them, but he that hath it, and hath power to act it." *

Moreover, faith secures our victory over the evil

---

* John Bunyan.

influences which beset us, by causing the world to appear as it really is. Oftentimes it appears otherwise. It assumes an undue attractiveness and importance; and then we are tempted to love it, and grasp it. But faith strips it of its tinsel and glitter, and exposes its deceitfulness and absolute nothingness. When the eye of faith is undimmed, and the Christian, from his proper elevation, looks down upon the honors, riches, and pleasures of earth, how fade they into insignificance! "To him who has ascended a mountain, the inequalities of the valley are all reduced to a plain; the men who are seen here and there hurrying through the rounds of business and pleasure, appear like so many children, and their thousand cares, their joys and sorrows, seem like so many childish vanities. So the Christian, *in the exercise of faith*, looks upon those things which formerly engaged his attention with comparative indifference. Riches, honors, pleasures, all appear unworthy of supreme regard; the elevations which men toil to reach, look petty and insignificant; the anxieties and fears with which they distress themselves, seem unworthy of one in whose behalf God himself is enlisted, and who has in sure reversion an eternal weight of glory."

So also does it effect this by bringing into close proximity the world to come. Heaven is near when we have strong faith. This telescope of the soul presents our blessed inheritance with wonderful distinctness. We seem verily to hear the "echoes of its rapturous songs;" and are ravished at beholding the glories of the "King Immortal," — the majesty of his person, and the magnificence of his retinue, the myriads of joyful, shining ones that bask in eternal light, and the unfading crowns, and harps of gold, and surpassing glory, that shall be ours when we join the blessed company.

What becomes of earth when we have such a view of heaven? Does it longer fill the mind, and draw upon the affections? Glowworms are bright in the absence of the sun; but when the great luminary lifts himself into view, glowworms, and moon, and stars disappear! So does our future glorious abode, as seen by the eye of faith, shine into darkness all the brightest objects of sense. Living in the world, by faith we live above the world. We trample it beneath our feet. We are neither elated by its prosperity, nor crushed by its adversity. Smiles, caresses, pleasures, — perils, persecutions, sword, nakedness, — none of these things move us, trusting in the Lord, and dwelling in perpetual light: —

> " As some tall cliff, that rears its awful form,
> Swells from the vale and midway leaves the storm, —
> Though round its breast the rolling clouds are spread,
> Eternal sunshine settles on its head."

We have now developed the nature, and traced some of the effects of that "*faith in God*" which constituted a peculiar feature in the piety of primitive times.

Does the faith which now prevails answer to this Scriptural standard? Does it give reality to unseen things? Does it answer to the "*substance*" of those things, and cause them powerfully to influence us, as if seen by the natural eyes? Is it the source of *happiness* to God's children? Are they remarkable, in any degree, for their constant joy and rejoicing in the Lord? Does it effect their *sanctification?* Does it lead them to "put off the old man with his deeds, and put on the new man, which is renewed in knowledge after the image of him who created him?" Does it impart Christian *boldness?* — a heroism that falters not before any kind or amount of opposition encountered in leading a life of eminent holiness? Does it also impart *activity* and *strength?* Is there vigor and manliness in Christian character, generally? And, finally, does it give us the victory over the world? Is it "an energizing, all-conquering principle, actually subordinating earthly things to heavenly?" If the faith that now obtains answers to this description, then is it a *scriptural* faith. If not, then is it defective. Does it answer to this description?

The question scarcely needs a formal answer. Who can take an intelligent view of the churches as they exist, and avoid the painful conviction that such a faith, to say the very least, is the *exception,* not the rule?

The narrow scale upon which our missionary enterprises are prosecuted, the low state of piety in the churches, and the limited accessions to their numbers, the want of simplicity of purpose, and of harmonious coöperation; the lack of personal consecration, and of self-denial for Christ; in a word, the inactivity of Christians in things spiritual, and their absorbing interest in things temporal, too plainly justify, as applicable to the followers of Christ in our day, his rebuke to one of old: "O thou of little faith, wherefore didst thou doubt?"

There is a vast deal of scepticism in the church. We do not mean theoretical merely, but practical and real; for it often occurs that our practice belies our theory. Professedly, we believe in prayer, but how much of narrowness and doubtfulness is there in our petitions, which we may imagine bespeaks humility, but which, in truth, betrays our "contemptuous unbelief!" How many fathers and mothers would be taken by surprise, should God suddenly come and convert their children, for whose conversion they have offered so many prayers! And how frequently are members of our churches, who have been heard to pray, in every petition which they have publicly offered for years, that God would revive his work, found lifting up their hands in astonishment, when once the shower of divine grace descends! In such cases, what is the conclusion? Certainly this; they *did not expect* that their prayers would be answered. From the duty of prayer, turn to that of giving the gospel to the heathen. In theory, we believe that the nations of the earth are Christ's; and that they are to be saved through the gospel.

But with regard to the whole matter of missions, how much is there of doubt and misgiving! The prevalence of scepticism in the church in respect to the facts and principles on which the work of missions proceeds, as one has ably maintained, is the main hindrance to the immediate evangelization of the world.* "The last hope of Satan," it is justly

* See Prelim. Essay to "Foster on Missions," by Rev. J. P Thompson.

added, "is in the timidity and doubtfulness of the church. He scatters distrust and fear among God's people. They hesitate, they fall back. Their scepticism checks the auspicious onset, prolongs the reign of darkness, abandons the world to guilt and wretchedness; and while God would give a triumph to heaven and a millennium to earth, this gives a jubilee to hell!" But why need we particularize? In what department of Christian duty is there not apparent a want of simple, childlike confidence in God, and earnest devotedness to the work of Christ's kingdom, as seen in primitive times?

The possession of such a faith is entirely practicable. There is nothing to sustain the too prevalent opinion that the faith of the early Christians is not to be expected in our day,—that Christ's simple promise—the staff on which leaned the primitive saints—is now obsolete or insufficient; a fitting remembrancer of other days, but not to be solely relied upon in the times in which we live. To *us*, as well as to those of any age, are all the promises "yea and amen in Christ Jesus;" and it is the privilege of every disciple so to interpret them, and act upon them.

The possession of such a faith is a cardinal necessity of any age. It was never more needful than at the present moment. We are too much inclined to consider the necessity of the faith of the martyr age as now passed. That in *other* days a heroic, self-forgetful assurance was requisite, is readily perceived; but we secretly excuse ourselves from efforts towards its attainment, from an apprehension that it is not *now* required.

What is there to justify this conclusion? Is not the "flesh" just as inimical to the "Spirit" now, as in the days when the apostle described its warrings against the gracious principle within? Is Satan less the Christian's adversary now than in other days? Is he less *malignant*, — less artful, — less assiduous in practising his "devices?" And the influence of surrounding objects, — is it less liable to contaminate and destroy? Has human nature become less selfish and depraved? Have ungodly men ceased their opposition to Christ, and his doctrines, and his disciples? Has the offence of the cross ceased?

> 'Is this vile world a friend to grace,
> To help us on to God?'

Let it not be believed. It is not the world that has become modified in favor of the church; but the church in favor of the world. Christian character assumes a less positive and decided stamp. The same unworldliness on the part of Christ's followers, — the same degree of faithfulness and holy living, — would provoke as great opposition now as was manifested in earlier times; though the form in which that opposition would appear might not be the same. Besides this, there are the same temptations now as ever before, — the same "lust of the flesh," and "lust of the eyes," and "pride of life," — the same fear of man which bringeth a snare; and the same corrupt maxims in moral, social, commercial, and political life. Who will allege, then, that primitive faith is not a requisite of our times?

We have seen, in a previous chapter, that there is now a fearful absence of *self-denial* for Christ. But *courage* is required to practise this virtue, — a courage kindred to that evinced in the age of persecutions. And to impart this courage, *faith* is necessary. Without it the individual falters at the thought of breasting the tide of worldliness, and appearing "singular" among men for his strict adherence to gospel principles.

As we have said, substantially, of self-denial, so we now say of faith; to overcome the world, — to rise above its temptations, to eschew its false maxims, to meet its hatred and contempt for Christ's sake, and to crucify the flesh, with its affections and lusts, and live soberly, righteously, and godly in the midst of a wicked and perverse generation, — to do *this*, requires a faith precisely *the same* in nature, and oftentimes in *degree*, with that possessed by the earlier Christians, who maintained their religion at the cost of their lives. For the want of it the type of piety has sadly deteriorated, — the followers of Christ becoming conformed to the world, and subject to its dictation as respects their rules and principles of life. O for the return of a primitive faith! Where are the Noahs, the Abrahams, the Nehemiahs, the Daniels, the Pauls of other days? Where a Moses, — esteeming the reproach of Christ greater riches than the treasures of Egypt? Where are the *women* who shall witness for Christ as in the martyr age? who will *insist*, — no matter with how much womanly dignity and discretion, — but who will *insist* that Christianity shall control the fashions, and *not* the fashions Christianity. Women have been willing to *die* for Christ:

who now will be willing to *live* for him; so that fashions and fashionable follies shall no longer drain the treasuries of wealth, till nothing is left for the conversion of the world?

We repeat it; a more Scriptural faith *must* prevail among the disciples of Jesus, before the glories of the millennium shall appear. Let earnest and continuous efforts be made, therefore, in this direction. Let the ministers of Christ hold up in contrast the present with the faith of earlier days. Let the members of the churches use the appointed means for a large increase of this heavenly grace.

It may be increased. Paul has hope of his brethren when "*their faith is increased.*" Is it asked, How shall its growth be secured? We answer; not without prayer. Here, as elsewhere, the law obtains, "Seek and ye shall find;" "ask and it shall be given unto you." But something besides prayer is necessary. It must be sought *by giving ourselves wholly to the Lord*, to do and suffer his will without reserve. In proportion as we *consecrate* ourselves to God, and live near unto him, shall we have confidence in him.

Our faith grows exceedingly, by the constant and *careful study of God's Word.* Revelation is the basis of faith. That is a beautiful conception of the sacred poet,—the placing beneath the arm of faith the volume of inspiration:—

"And faith stands *leaning on his word.*"

Christian confidence is weak and tremulous because it is not, by much devout meditation, made to settle and rest firmly upon the divine promises. Replete as are the Scriptures with precisely such truths as are adapted to support and strengthen our faith, by becoming, to a greater extent, its uniform and prayerful students, more of vigor and stability cannot but be given to this heavenly grace.

Faith is also increased by its *exercise.* It is said that the surest remedy for short-sightedness, is the continued practice of endeavoring, by a steady effort of the eye, to get a sight of objects at a distance. The practised eye of him who has long been wont to gaze upon the heavens and count the stars, discovers new bodies the more it stretches forth its vision to detect them, until thousands are seen which the untrained eye of other men cannot behold. Even so it is of the eye of faith. Its capacity is enlarged by use. Every exercise, on the part of the believer, of a far-reaching faith, prepares him the better for its subsequent exercise.

Or, to use a different and borrowed illustration, "As the earthly warrior is not made such by the holiday parade merely, the epaulette, and the nodding plume, and the fluttering of silken standards, but by the dust and toil of the actual field, and by the agony of the strife and the death-grapple; so the heroes of faith become such, not by mere profession, or large knowledge, or solemn rite, but by fighting manfully the good fight of faith, armed with the whole armor of God, and resisting in the name and strength of the Captain of their salvation, sin unto the death."

By these, and by all other means, let Christians strive to go from strength to strength in this grace, walking "in the steps of that faith of our father

Abraham." And when this shall be generally found true of Christ's followers; when they shall come to believe what God has spoken, and simply because he has spoken it; when they shall fall back upon the divine promises, and ceasing from man, hang their hopes upon the pillars of the everlasting throne; when, in a word, they are become "strong in faith," and through its victories have overcome the world, *then* what beauty and power shall invest our holy religion! What an earthly embodiment of heavenly perfections! What love and purity and zeal and godliness! Blessed with spiritual light and life,—rooted and grounded in the faith,—cleansed from inward corruption,—Christians shall no more "live at this poor dying rate," but, growing in grace and in the knowledge of God, attain unto the stature of perfect men in Christ Jesus. Then shall they think less of earth and more of heaven; less of their own ease, or honors, or misfortunes, and more of the interests of the Redeemer's kingdom. Then the channels of Christian benevolence shall be swollen with the contributions of cheerful givers; because, taking hold upon the pledge of Jehovah, that those that wait upon the Lord shall not want any good thing, and that seeking first the kingdom of God and his righteousness all other things shall be added, the saints of the Most High will seek to accumulate but that they may have wherewith to feed the hungry, clothe the naked, and give the gospel to the destitute. Then, *what answers to prayer!* Instead of asking "amiss," and receiving not, with this firm assurance in the veracity of the Promiser, we should "ask in faith, nothing wavering;" and find fulfilled the promise, " Whatsoever ye ask, in prayer, *believing*, ye shall receive."

And then what unremitted exertion to save dying men! How many of the members of the churches are now living, year after year, with almost no direct efforts to save souls. How many children of professedly pious parents have yet to be conversed and prayed with by those parents for *the first time!* How many domestics and clerks and apprentices in the employ of Christian professors, are altogether unwarned and uninstructed in religion! How *few* of those who bear the name of Christ, as they meet and mingle with the unconverted are pained at their guilt and danger, and watching and laboring for their salvation! And why? Because the truths of religion are dimly perceived; and cannot, therefore, affect the mind and incite to action.

O, were we to stand, for one brief hour, at the verge of the pit, where

> " There are groans that end not, and sighs
> That always sigh, and tears that ever weep,
> And ever fall, but not in mercy's sight,"

would it be *possible* for us to remain unmoved?

Now a faith like that described would serve in room of the literal facts. It would give to things unseen all the freshness and reality which attach to objects seen with the natural eye. Possessed of this faith, the bliss of heaven, the prisonhouse of hell, the judgment throne, *all* the great facts of a future just before us, would seem like facts, and like them impel to action. Under its influence the husband and parent would ponder in anticipation, the trial at the last great day, of a companion or child, now out of Christ, and the awful sentence of "depart, ye cursed;" and the *actual sight* could not affect him more. He would weep and pray; he would exhort and entreat; he would not, he *could* not rest until the loved object had fled for refuge to Christ.

And so with regard to *every thing* connected with religion. We do not act until we *feel*, and we cannot feel until we *believe*. A pusillanimous and inert faith underlies all this inactivity and unconcern, on the part of Christians, touching the perishing condition of dying men around them. The remedy for this, and, to a great extent, for all the evils that afflict the church of Christ, is therefore obvious. It is an enlarged and vigorous faith. We must put away our distrust. O this wicked unbelief which is our besetting sin!

If the Roman army lost a single victory because the numerous mice that infested the country had gnawed their bowstrings, how many a victory has been lost by the soldiers of the cross because the sinews of their spiritual strength had been cut by the sins of unbelief?

"Ah, my friends," exclaimed the venerable Miller, "the lack of faith is the great, crying sin, not of an ungodly world only, but eminently of Christians. It is the littleness of our faith which makes us dwarfs in spiritual stature; cowards in conflict and in enterprise; narrow-minded in our views and plans of duty; and niggards in sacrifice and in contribution to the cause of Christ. Yes, it is the sin and the misery even of the sincere disciples of Christ, that the promises of God have so little daily influence on their practical habits. Christians! be afraid of unbelief; be ashamed of unbelief; only believe, and act as if you believed; and you shall see the salvation of God."*

Before dismissing this subject, dear reader, make it a matter of personal application. Propose to yourself such questions as these: 'Do I possess a Scriptural faith?' 'Is mine a faith that works by love, and purifies the heart, and overcomes the world?' 'Does it govern my affections, and direct my will, and rule my conduct, and lead me to live as a pilgrim and stranger upon earth?' Be entreated to seek the larger acquisition of such a faith. Bring it into daily exercise; foster its development; and often present yourself at the Saviour's feet with the earnest supplication, "*Increase my faith!*"

---

* Rev. Samuel Miller, D.D., in sermon at the 26th Anniversary of the American Board of Commissioners for Foreign Missions.

CHAPTER VI.

FIFTH GRAND DEFECT — A WANT OF EARNESTNESS.

Xavier's Night Vision. — The earnest Man. — The earnest Christian. — Christ an Example of Earnestness. — Paul. — The Order of the Jesuits. — The "United Brethren." — The Achievements of Earnestness. — To what Extent it obtains among Christians in this Age. — Necessity of Increase. — In the Ministry. — Power of Earnestness. — Want of it acknowledged. — John Welch. — John Knox. — Earnest Laymen required. — Regard for Themselves requires it. — Suitable Care for Others. — The Spirit of the Age makes this essential. — Contrast between Earnestness of the World and the Church. — Vigor within necessary to resent Evils from without. — Ancient Church; how corrupted. — Present Danger from Wickedness in High Places, — from Romanism and from Formalism. — Deterioration already commenced. — Address to the Reader.

When Xavier was preparing to go forth upon his mission through the East, his friend Rodriguez, who shared his apartment in the Hospital at Rome, was awakened in the night by his earnest exclamations. He heard him tossing restlessly on his couch; and at times there came from the lips of the sleeping man the agitated appeal, "Yet more, O my God! yet more!"

It was not until many months afterwards, that he revealed the vision. He had seen in his slumber the wild and terrible future of his career spread out before him. There were barbarous regions, islands, and continents, and mighty empires which he was to win to his faith. Storms, indeed, swept around them, and hunger and thirst were everywhere, and death in many a fearful form; yet he shrank not back. He was willing to dare the peril, if he could but win the prize. Nay, he yearned for still wider fields of labor, and with an absorbing passion, that filled every faculty, and haunted him even in his slumber, he exclaimed, "*Yet more, O my God! yet more!*"* The incident furnishes a fine illustration of Christian earnestness.

Earnestness is ardor or zeal in pursuit of any object. The earnest man is full of longing desire; he is warmly engaged, and eager to obtain that which he seeks. He is ever urging and pressing toward it, and cannot rest satisfied so long as he falls short of it. The earnest man is a man of courage, and faith, and patience, and constancy. He is not easily diverted from his purpose. Having determined his end, and the means of accomplishing it, he can neither be drawn nor driven aside. On, *on* he presses, yearning and struggling still, till that end is attained.

The earnest Christian is one who is ardently incited, and strongly determined about the things of godliness. There is force in his character, and life and fire. He is not a sluggish, indolent Christian; but is impelled by the energies of a wakeful, active mind. He stands firmly by his principles, and battles dauntlessly for God and the truth. He is powerfully under the influence of religious things, and is

* See Kip's Conflicts of Christianity, pp. 185 186.

animated and borne onward by intense zeal for the interests of Christ's kingdom. Earnestness, in the Christian, is, therefore, the prime element of success. Destitute of this, what is he? what does he accomplish? The principles of religion do not take strong hold upon him, and he has little courage to defend them, and still less disposition to practise them, when it is at the cost of any considerable sacrifice. His religion is of a weak, negative character; it is puny, sickly, lifeless, and inoperative. And this element of character is everywhere recognized in the Scriptures, as thus essential to success.

Hence we are *earnestly* to contend for the faith once delivered to the saints. We are to covet *earnestly* the best gifts; and to *do with our might* what our hands find to do. Without it *prayer* avails not. The prophet "prayed *earnestly* that it might not rain," and it rained not for the space of three years and six months. Jacob *wrestled* with the Angel; and the disciples made prayer "without ceasing," or instant and earnest prayer, as it reads in the margin, for imprisoned Peter, who was forthwith delivered by the angel. And it is the fervent prayer of the righteous that is effectual and avails much.

How bright an example of earnestness in religion is furnished us in the life of Christ! It marked his career from Nazareth to the Cross. 'His zeal for his Father's house devoured him.' Like a sacred flame glowing in his bosom, it preyed upon his spirits. His was a life of unceasing and untiring activity. We always find him, look where we will, "working, preaching, praying, or weeping, but never loitering."

He was *intent* on the object that filled his eye, his heart, his hands,—the saving of souls. His meat and his drink was to do his Father's will. His relaxation was devotion; and though "all the fulness and fire of the passions dwelt in him, never did he waste a single feeling, but devoted the whole as consecrated fuel for offering up the great sacrifice in which his life was consumed, and by which the world might be saved!" How careful is he to make the most of every moment! The disciples are gone away to the city to buy provision; but though hungry and thirsty, he eagerly seizes upon the fragment of time, and instructs and enlightens and saves the woman of Samaria. He enters the humble and quiet mansion of his favorite friends in Bethany. Is it not to seek a little repose after so much exhausting toil? Will he not rest, at least, until the body is refreshed by food? Instead of this, on entering the house, he at once enters upon "his Master's business." From the posture of Mary, sitting as a pupil at his feet, and listening to his words, as well as from his gentle reproof of Martha, for her excess of anxiety to entertain liberally her Lord, it is obvious that he had immediately before the repast, engaged in the work of carefully unfolding and illustrating some great truth of his holy religion.

And so at all times, and in all places, He is possessed with the magnitude of his task; he is eager for its accomplishment. "I have a baptism to be baptized with," he exclaimed, "and how am I straitened till it is accomplished." It has been remarked of him, that his eagerness for man's salvation was such that the guilty heart of the traitor was too slow in its purpose for his love, and he quickened the movements of Judas by those memorable words, "What thou doest, do quickly." He made haste to the cross. He was almost impatient for the hour of sacrifice. He could brook no delay in love's redeeming work. O what an example of *earnestness* in regard to the things of eternity!

And next in brightness to the example of our Lord, stands that of his servant Paul. His conversion and history seem "designed to teach us what energy may be compressed into one human heart, to be developed in one single life." So earnest was he in the work of saving men, that he indited to them his epistles while "weeping;" and 'ceased not to warn every one, night and day, with tears.' He ceased not; he did it night and day; and he did it *with tears!* And, testifying of himself, he declares, "For me to live is Christ." What an epitome of his whole character and life; perhaps best paraphrased by another thus: "Christ is my life: apart from him and his work I seem to have no separate existence: I have grown into that one object."

At Corinth, waiting for the coming of Silas and Timotheus, he "was pressed in the spirit, and testified that Jesus was Christ." At Athens, too, he waited for them; and in the interim, what are his thoughts and feelings, and in what do we find him engaged? He had been familiar with the fame of that city; but this, so far as we know, was the first time he had ever visited it. Bred in a city whose "schools rivalled those of Athens," read in the Grecian classics, he would surely be both qualified and inclined to examine its things of beauty and renown with his own eyes. He might now for the first, perhaps for the last time, behold those schools, and academic groves, and works of art, which were, and in part still are, the admiration of the world. But did he yield to a most natural inclination? Did he suffer any of these things to absorb, even for a day, his time and attention? A few words tell the whole story: "Now while Paul waited for them at Athens, his spirit was stirred within him when he saw the city wholly given to idolatry: therefore disputed he in the synagogue with the Jews, — and in the market, daily with them that met him." Ah! there he is; that is his employment for a few "leisure hours," as most men would have called them; arguing, instructing, exhorting, with the object of saving souls!

And thus it was everywhere. His self-consuming zeal forbade him to rest satisfied. He counted nothing gained till all was gained. He still cried, "Yet *more!* O my God, *yet* MORE!" or, in his own language, "having hope . . . that we shall be *enlarged* by you according to our rule abundantly, to preach the gospel in the regions beyond you." His soul was on fire when he thought of the cross and of a dying world. He would not, he could not refrain from effort. Ease might offer him indulgence; wealth might display her bribes; pleasure might exhibit her charms; persecution might bring out and spread in his path a fearful array of scourges, and chains, and axes; but he looked at the cross, and beholding the Son of God suspended there, he armed himself, "likewise, with the same mind." He looked around and he saw the assembled church of Jesus Christ urging him, for the glory of the cross, and for perishing humanity, to go forward. He looked above, and saw a great "cloud of witnesses" bending with intent interest from their blessed seats; and beyond and above them all, he saw the throne of the Lamb and him that sat upon it, and in his extended hand a glorious crown of life; and thus impelled he led the van of the army of the cross, and stormed the strong-holds of Satan and sin, exulting, with the song of a Christian warrior, "Now thanks be unto God, who always causeth us to triumph in every place!"

Others of primitive times might be instanced as examples of earnestness in Christ's service; for who has failed to remark the absolute, vigorous character of the early piety, and the absorbing, all-controlling passion for saving souls, which seemed to be generally possessed? And to this is unquestionably attributable, to a great extent, the rapid spread of Christianity in the first few centuries.

Approaching our own times, we meet with a remarkable class of men — the order of Jesuits — whose entire history is a striking commentary upon the subject under consideration. It was an apparently unimportant transaction, the taking of a solemn vow at the midnight hour, by Ignatius Loyola and his few companions, in the chapel of the abbey of Montmartre near Paris, a little more than three centuries ago, — by which vow they bound themselves to renounce the world for the purpose of preaching the gospel. But who can tell how deeply the plans and efforts of those seven poor students and their successors have affected the history, and shall yet affect the destiny of Europe, and Asia, and Africa, and America? What spot upon the world has not felt their influence? Had they disseminated the pure gospel of Christ, instead of the delusions of Antichrist, the nations of the earth had been, before this, evangelized.

But what is the secret of their prodigious, far reaching influence? What but their indomitable perseverance, their stout, earnest hearts; their zeal, their burning enthusiasm, which those of a purer faith might well emulate?

At the command of the pope, said Ignatius, 'I would embark on a mission for any shore, in a vessel without rudder, sails, mast, or stores. And in imitation of his zeal, the entire order were keyed to a pitch of moral heroism, such as never existed in any other equally large company of men.

"In all their missions," says one who has ably sketched their history, "the order displayed an indomitable energy, and a spirit of most adventurous enterprise. As dauntless as they were versatile, and as unwearied as they were dauntless, the door closed against them was undermined, if it could not be opened, and stormed where it could not be undermined. Martyrdom had for them no terrors. Did the news return to their colleges in Europe of a missionary falling riddled by the arrows of a Brazilian savage, at the foot of the crucifix he had planted, or of scores sent into the depths of the ocean by heretic captors, the names of the fallen were inserted on the rubrics of Jesuit martyrs; and not the students only, but the professors of their institutions, rushed to fill the ranks that had been thus thinned."* Of

* The Jesuits as a missionary order: Christian Review, 1841

an earnestness such as this, was not their wonderful success almost a natural result?

Turn next to the "United Brethren," or Moravians, as they are called; who began their missionary operations when their whole society numbered only about six hundred persons, and they, chiefly were poor exiles.

As a single instance of the uniform ardor and energy with which their work is prosecuted, mention might be made of the planting of a mission in Greenland in 1733. The pioneers of that enterprise were three illiterate men, Christian David, and two brothers, whose names were Matthew and Christian Stark. They had heard that the people of Greenland had no knowledge of the Saviour; and with almost no outfit, they were upon the wearisome journey to teach them the way of salvation. Arrived at Copenhagen, having travelled thither on foot, their project was ridiculed as romantic and impracticable. They were informed that they could not live there; that the country affording no wood, they could not even build a house to live in. "Oh, then we will dig in the earth and live *there;*" was their only reply. On reaching the place of their destination, for want of employment as a means of support, they began the business of spinning. To acquire the language of the natives, it was first necessary to acquire that of their instructor. This task,—to them most difficult from their ignorance of the laws of language,—once overcome, the severity of their labors, and the extremity of their wants exposed them to the attacks of disease, and brought them wellnigh to the grave. And what was more, they saw no fruit of their labor. For five long, tedious years, not a solitary conversion was witnessed. But yet, recruited by the arrival of two other missionaries, they toil on in the spirit of their motto, "We will believe, though there be nothing to be seen; and we will hope, though there be nothing to be expected;" and, in due time, their hearts are gladdened with the results of their earnest and self-sacrificing efforts.

> "Fired with a zeal peculiar, they defy
> The rage and vigor of a northern sky;
> And plant successfully, sweet Sharon's rose
> On icy plains, and in eternal snows."

It has been recently stated that the living converts of the "United Brethren," number nearly eighteen thousand, and they are found in almost all parts of the world. And all this is the result, under God, of a comparatively few earnest, resolute minds.

Indeed, what will not a mind, charged with downright earnestness, accomplish? Whether we discover the force of this principle in the things of this world, as when it impels a Newton to pore over his problems "till the midnight wind swept over his papers the ashes of his long extinguished fire," — or a Reynolds to hold in hand his pencil for thirty-six hours together, — or a Dryden to think on, for a fortnight, in a perfect frenzy, when composing an ode, heedless of privations, even, which he did not so much as perceive, — or a Heyne, the German scholar, to allow himself "no more than two nights of weekly rest," for six months in succession, that he might complete the perusal of old Greek authors; or, whether we discover it in the concerns of religion, — as when it urged on Martin Luther in his gigantic labors of preaching, journeying, debating, corresponding, and book writing, until, at the time of his death, the number of works he had published was seven hundred and fifteen, or more than twenty-five for each year of his public life, and the visible results of other labors beyond estimate or description, — or William Carey to think, and ponder, and study, and weep, and preach, and pray about the poor heathen, until the ocean separated him from his native land; and then to toil and struggle in the dark habitations of cruelty, until he had furnished for more than three hundred millions of immortal beings the "golden lamp of heaven," — or John Wesley to preach, and study, and write, and travel five thousand miles a year, and "read on horseback, history, poetry, philosophy," — or George Whitefield to exclaim at the close of his first sermon, "Glorious God!

> "Unloose my stammering tongue to tell
> Thy love immense, unsearchable,"

and, for thirty-four years, to traverse England, Ireland, and Scotland, and cross the Atlantic Ocean thirteen times, preaching everywhere and at all times the gospel of God's grace, — or Howard, to penetrate the haunts of poverty and disease, watch over sick and dying criminals, plunge into clammy dungeons where reigned madness and death, and sacrifice his life in deeds of philanthropy, — or a Clarkson, to lay aside "the vestments of the priesthood," and with his few fellow workers plead for twenty years for the suffering sons of Africa, until "the cry of the oppressed roused the sensibilities of the nation, and the 'Island Empress' rose in her might, and said to the foul traffic in human flesh, Thus far shalt thou go, and no further," — wherever it is observed, it seems to clothe one with a kind of omnipotence. We expect little from the *opposite* character, the sluggish, irresolute man, but *here* we always anticipate important results.

And *to what extent does this principle obtain among the mass of professing Christians in our day?* That they do not generally evince, in matters of religion, any thing like the zeal which is required in order to the largest success of the gospel, is universally acknowledged and deplored. The sentiment of Rev. John Angel James, in his excellent work, "The Church in Earnest," will meet with a general affirmative response: "He must have formed very inadequate ideas of what is necessary for the conversion of a world from sin and Satan to Christ and holiness, who imagines this will ever be done without the most intense earnestness, and a degree of self-devotement which has never been witnessed, except in a comparatively few instances, since the days of the apostles. . . . . Let any one imagine what a triumph over all the selfishness, the cupidity, the worldliness, the indolence, the luxuriousness which are to be found among professors, must take place; and what a preponderance of the holy, heavenly, spiritual, self-denying, generous virtues must come on, — what a general breaking down of all the barriers of prejudice between different denominations of Christians must be effected, — what a fair and open field for the operations of Christian zeal must be presented, — what a mighty growth of spiritual power from all sections of the one church must be exhibited, — before ever these realms of darkness and wickedness are evangelized. What a great work it must be to overtake the population of even this country with the means of religious instruction, and to reclaim from sterility and desolation the vast and neglected wastes which are found here; and to drain and cultivate these pestilent bogs of ignorance, crime, and misery! And this is only but as the homestead, and the garden, compared with the wilderness of Paganism and Mohammedanism that lies beyond. Let any man cast his eye over a map of our globe, with a geographical and historical knowledge of the tyrannical governments, the idolatrous religions, the savage barbarism, the multifarious languages, the unapproachable suspicion, which are comprehended under the names and within the lines that are before him; and think of winning all this to Christ, and covering all these dark domains of sin and Satan with the beauties of holiness, the joys of hope, the blessings of salvation, — and yet this is the business of the church, its labor and its hope. Will these valleys be filled up, these mountains be levelled? Will these crooked things be made straight, and these rough places be made plain, without an earnestness we have never yet witnessed? Is there not an agonizing effort, such as we know nothing about, yet to be called forth, by which all this is to be achieved? We have even yet to learn what kind of work we have undertaken in setting our hands to the world's conversion; and must be made to learn, perhaps, more painfully, more impressively, than we have yet done, the nature of the difficulties that are to be overcome, that we may see what kind of men, and what kind of efforts, are required for the accomplishment of the marvellous and glorious consummation."

There should be an increased earnestness in the *ministry* of our day. Allusion has been made to the heroic devotedness and self-consuming zeal of the Apostle to the Gentiles. But is he not too often considered, in this respect, as beyond imitation? Does not doubt oftentimes exist as to whether it could reasonably be expected of modern ministers to be as intensely and wholly absorbed in the work of the Master as was Paul? And yet is it anywhere even intimated that he was to be considered as an exception to what others should be? Nay, is not a construction of his example such as this, plainly forbidden by his own words, "Be ye followers of me, even as I also am of Christ?" It must be admitted, therefore, that the example of the apostle furnishes a model to which ministers of the gospel, in all time, may and should conform. And can it be doubted that, because, in respect to an entire self-devotement, the ministry at large are not followers of him who so closely followed Christ, they are not to a greater extent sharers of his success? Were their labors marked by the same earnestness, would they not also be attended with the same or similar blessed results?

"Ministers," said the excellent John Sutcliff, "ministers will never do much good till they begin to pull sinners out of the fire." Is there enough of this laying hold upon ungodly men, and plucking them as brands from the burning? Is there enough of beseeching men, *with tears*, night and day, to be reconciled to God? Is there not too often a resting satisfied with the mere *routine* of duty, — with an attendance to the prescribed forms or engagements, in an *ex officio* manner, the *heart* not being in the work, and the *will not intently set upon achieving some worthy result?* It is to be feared this is too much the case in the public ministration of the Word. The mind does not, in all cases, glow with the subject under consideration, — it does not fill the soul, and warm into life its emotions.

"Who is likely," asks one, "to be moved by hearing a man discuss the most awful realities of eternal truth, such as the danger and the doom of immortal souls, the glories of heaven, and the torments of hell, with as much coolness, and with as little emotion as a lecturer on science would exhibit when dwelling on the facts of natural history?" Unless the preacher feel, how can it be expected that the hearer should feel? There is much force in the well-known reply of the actor to the minister who inquired, "How is it that your performances, which are but pictures of the imagination, produce so much more effect than our sermons, which are all realities?" "Because," said the actor, "we represent our fictions as though they were realities, and you preach your realities as though they were fictions."

Taylor informs us, that when Loyola commenced his discourse, a breathless silence reigned through the church; and that as he proceeded there was perceptible pressure towards the pulpit; sighs soon became audible on every side; then these sighs swelled into sobs, and these sobs into groans. Some fell on the pavements as if lifeless. Once and again an obdurate offender — hitherto obdurate — pushed forward, threw himself at the feet of the preacher as he left the pulpit, and with convulsive struggles made a loud confession of his crimes. And he adds, that men from every class of society, not exclusive of dignified ecclesiastics, "were numbered among the conquests of earnest preaching."

"I have not wept but once these forty years," said a veteran military officer, "and that was when I heard Jesse Busheyhead, the Cherokee preacher, address his countrymen from the parable of the prodigal son, the tears flowing faster than he could wipe them away."

An unopened note was found upon the table of McCheyne, after his death, from one who heard his last sermon, to this effect: "Pardon a stranger for addressing to you a few lines. I heard you preach last Sabbath evening, and it pleased God to bless that sermon to my soul. It was not so much *what* you said, as the *manner* of speaking it that struck me. I saw in you a beauty of holiness I never saw before." He who has read the life and writings of this young servant of Christ, and marked his earnest, loving, melting appeals, can readily account for this effect upon the stranger's mind.

And is there any thing remarkable in all this? Is not *love* "the key to the human soul?" Does it not give access to hearts? One may meet logic, and smile at rhetoric, and be unmoved by eloquence; but *can* he resist *love?* Can he see one deeply intent upon his salvation, — distressed about his dangerous condition, pleading, urging, entreating, weeping, praying,—and all with a view to his benefit, and remain unaffected? "Why is he so anxious about *me?*" is the involuntary suggestion. "I cannot stand this earnestness." "If he is so concerned about my soul, surely I ought to be concerned about myself." "There must be a *reality* in what he says, or he could not be so deeply moved." Thus it is in every department of ministerial labor. Earnestness is the pledge of success,—its absence renders it impossible.

The world has little to hope from men, says one, "*merely* because they happen to occupy the pulpit, instead of some other position,—merely because they are *Reverends*, instead of *Judges* and *Generals*." The source of hope is in the *earnest workers*. It was for "*laborers*" in the harvest-field that our Lord taught his disciples to pray; and many, according to their own painful convictions, come far short in ardent, laborious, self-sacrificing effort in the work of gathering souls to Christ. Baxter is not the only one who could say, "I confess, to my shame, that I remember no one sin that my conscience doth so much accuse and judge me for, as for doing so little for the salvation of men's souls, and dealing no more earnestly and fervently with them for their conversion. I confess that when I am alone, and think of the case of poor, ignorant, worldly, earthly, unconverted sinners, that live not to God nor set their hearts on the life to come, my conscience telleth me that I should go to as many of them as I can, and tell them plainly what will become of them if they do not turn; and beseech them with all the earnestness that I can, to come to Christ, and change their course, and make no delay. And though I have many excuses, from other business, and from disability and want of time, yet none of them all do satisfy my own conscience when I consider what heaven and hell are, which will one of them be the end of every man's life. My conscience telleth me that I should follow them with all possible earnestness, night and day, and take no denial till they turn to God." It is more of this *beseeching* men to turn to God, and taking no denial, this *setting of the heart upon it*, and feeling a sadness, a "continual sorrow" until their salvation is secure, it is *this* that is required.

John Welch used to keep a plaid upon his bed that he might wrap himself in it when he arose in the night to pray. Sometimes his wife found him upon the ground weeping; and when she complained, he would say, "O woman, I have the souls of three thousand to answer for, and I know not how it is with many of them!" Akin to this was the spirit of John Knox, who was led to exclaim in a prayer for his beloved country, "O God, give me Scotland or I die!" Such was the spirit of David when he could say, "Rivers of water run down mine eyes because they keep not thy law;" and of Jeremiah, in uttering that pathetic exclamation, "O that my head were waters, and mine eyes a fountain of tears, that I might weep, day and night, for the slain of the daughter of my people!"—and of Paul, who thus gives expression to the "great heaviness" that pressed upon his soul; "I could wish that myself were accursed from Christ, for my brethren, my kinsmen according to the flesh!"

When all those who are specially called to watch for souls, shall have become possessed of this spirit,—when they shall be found thus intent upon the salvation of dying men,—how bright shall be the conquests of our King! Themselves impelled by ardent desires and high-born resolves, the people shall catch their spirit, and with an unwonted energy strike hands in doing battle for the "Lord of hosts." For it must be borne in mind, that not the ministers *only* but also the *people* have need of greater earnestness in the matters of religion.

A proper regard for their own salvation requires it. They must *strive* to enter in at the strait gate. They must "fight the good fight of faith" and "lay hold upon eternal life." And who does not discover that the prevailing disposition to smooth down the rougher points of religion, as they are termed, and make salvation an easier matter than it is represented in the Scriptures, as well as the almost unprecedented strife after wealth, and tendency on the part of professors of religion to become conformed to the world, render it absolutely essential that Christians be more deeply concerned and interested about their personal salvation? And there must be far more earnestness with regard to the salvation of others. A missionary to the heathen, in addressing his brethren at home, says: "To the Great Head of the church we must look for a *new order* of men,—men just as absorbed in winning souls to Christ, as worldlings are in gathering gold."

Ah, how merited the reproof implied in this language! *Are* Christians thus "absorbed" in the blessed service? Does it take hold upon their hearts and desires? Upon this one point do they concentrate all their enterprise? Would to God it were so! But "where," as one exclaims, "are the kindled eye, and the beaming countenance, and the heart bursting with the momentous importance of the gospel message? Where the fearlessness and confidence whose very tones inspire conviction, and carry with them all the force of certainty, and the weight of an oath? Where the zeal which burns with its subject, as if it had just come from witnessing the crucifixion, and felt its theme with all the freshness and force of a new revelation? — the zeal which, during its intervals of labor, repairs to the mount of vision, to see the funeral procession of six hundred millions of souls; to the mouth of hell, to hear six hundred millions of voices saying, as the voice of one man, 'Send to our brethren lest they also come to this place of torment;' to Calvary to renew its vigor by touching the cross; to the spot where John stood, to catch a view of the ranks of the blessed above.*

Some few instances of a zeal like this are witnessed, but, alas, *how* few! Considerations of the most weighty character demand that there be found among the followers of Christ, more of this ardent engagedness in the work to which they are called. It is rendered necessary by the *spirit of the age*, whose great characteristic is mental and social activity. The energies of men were never before so thoroughly awakened as at this moment. Everywhere are restlessness, change, enterprise, progress. The world is on tiptoe; the spirit of inquiry is abroad; and the forces of mankind are stimulated to their highest pitch.

In the affairs of life, *Christians* are as ardent and

---

* See "Witnessing Church," p. 64.

laborious as other men. There, they are intent upon their object. To compass their ends they rise early and sit up late. By day their eyes and ears are open, and their hands are filled with work; and by night, their thoughts are busy upon the best plans of business for the morrow. But how little of this deep interest and determined effort, on the part of Christians generally, with reference to advancing the glory of God in the world! How few minds study and plan by day and meditate by night, upon the problem, "What *can* be done to save men from perdition?" Alas, that here, just where they should feel most, here, where the things of the *soul*, and *God*, and *eternity* are involved, they are so listless, unconcerned, inactive!

The activity of which we speak sometimes manifests itself in *enterprise*, or bold, resolute, adventurous undertakings. And how much of this is observable in the things of this world! What comprehensiveness and keen calculation and far-sightedness in the laying of plans of action! What skill, and energy, and perseverance in carrying out those plans! The most subtle and powerful agencies *at any cost*, must be employed, and risks of property and life, even, scarcely taken into account, while instances of failure and defeat but render more intent the will, and determined the effort.

But how little enterprise is manifest in connection with the cause of Christ! Here the policy is cold, cautious, calculating. Here we walk *by sight*, and sacrifice zeal to prudence, which is, more properly speaking, timidity, or unbelief. As viewed by many, our faithful Master must not be trusted to too large an amount of money, and for too long a time, but we must be sure that we are *safe* at every single moment, and in the investment of every single dollar! O how sickening the contrast here, between things worldly and religious! With God on their side, and all the promises, it would seem that Christians might be more enterprising than the men of the world. Especially when we remember that in magnitude and glory, their work as far surpasses that of the worldling, as eternity surpasses time. But where we should expect to find the most of bold and high resolve, there we find the least.

The men of this world are wiser in their generation than the children of light. Shrewd, foresighted, adventurous in their operations, they realize large success. Mountains are tunnelled and reduced to plains, deep valleys are filled or bridged at immense expense, to form the iron or the watery way, the solid earth is encompassed with wiry lines for the lightning's course, and the great deep mapped out into thoroughfares and traversed for the commerce of the nations; and the returns are commensurate with the magnitude of their undertakings.

But where are the adventurers for Christ? How few are engrossed in projecting stupendous enterprises whereby a large revenue of glory shall accrue to the blessed Redeemer? How few are willing to run risks in bold, aggressive plans of benevolence! A missionary of the cross has well asked: "Is it not a fact that will strike us dumb at the judgment, that it is the love of money, not zeal for God, that digs canals, lays railroads, runs steamboats and packets, and, in short, is the mainspring in every great undertaking?" Why, oh why should not Christians be foremost in zeal and enterprise?

Always desirable, it is especially so in an age like this. An active piety is alone adapted to active times. An earnest spirit in the world, renders necessary an earnest spirit in the church. Unless it is possessed, the former, and not the latter, will take the lead in society; and facilities, such as an active age is sure to furnish for advancing the cause of Christ, will pass by unimproved. How imperative the demand, then, for earnest Christians; not ministers alone, but laymen, — men whose souls are deeply intent upon rendering the recent unprecedented progress in society, intelligence, and wealth, and discovery, and the remarkable revolutions and changes in the world, subservient to the interests of the kingdom of grace, — eager stockholders in noble Christian enterprises, — argus eyed men, watching for chances to gain some glorious end for Christ, and determined to trust and test God to the utmost. What wonders would even a few such men, under God, accomplish!

There is another consideration which gives emphasis to the demand of which we speak; namely, the *purity and prosperity of the church.* She needs force within in order to resist corrupting influences from without. For want of this, the ancient church lost her purity and strength. There was not internal vigor sufficient to repel the pernicious evils against which she at first contended, but which, at length, were allowed to insinuate themselves, in the form of Roman policy, and Gothic ignorance, and Grecian ingenuity, and Syrian asceticism. It must be apparent to every reflecting mind, that there are now evil influences in operation against the body of Christ's disciples, which can be repelled only by an increase of life and vigor within. One of these influences has been alluded to in a previous chapter. Look at others. The church is in danger of being corrupted by the wickedness of the times upon which we have fallen.

The language of Micah is peculiarly appropriate to our day: "The good man is perished out of the earth; and there is none upright among men: they all lie in wait for blood; they hunt every man his brother with a net. That they may do evil with both hands earnestly, the prince asketh, and the judge asketh for a reward; and the great man, he uttereth his mischievous desire; so they wrap it up." The example of wicked men is always pernicious; how much more so when it comes clothed with position and authority. When the fountains of influence are corrupt, it certainly requires the utmost exertion to keep the waters sweet. In the times of Israel the people were often rendered vile in the sight of God, through the defection of their rulers.

There is, after all, less to fear from wickedness in low places, than in high places; and if in our day there is a general and painful absence of integrity, and sound, high-toned morality among those who are prominent from their ambitious or selfish designs, or their official position, we may rest assured that the evil will diffuse itself downward throughout the various ramifications of society, and that the churches of Jesus Christ are in the highest danger of partaking of the general contamination. Their only safety is in a courageous, unflinching defence of the pure principles of the gospel; illustrating them in their daily conduct, and insisting upon their application to every possible grade and condition and relation of life. If any quarter is given to the godless, semi-infidel precepts of the day, — if Christians, through fear or favor, are induced partially to yield their ground, or in one single iota compromise their principles, consequences the most disastrous cannot fail to be the result. And they surely *will* yield unless their piety be of a vigorous, earnest character.

Moreover, the *acknowledged enemies* of a pure religion are intent upon the overthrow of Christ's church in the earth. Not to speak of disguised sceptics, and avowed rationalists and infidels, look at Romanists in our own and other lands. At one time thirty young priests sent a request to the Propaganda Society, with their names signed with blood drawn from their own veins, and requesting to be sent as missionaries to China. It is but a single illustration of the zeal with which our adversaries prosecute their work. Whether at the Vatican, — where gigantic intellects are planning and 'burning hearts are feeding the fire of their zeal,' and busy hands are working on daring and mischievous designs, — or in our own cities, — or on the missionary field, these emissaries of darkness are ever on the alert, impelled by a zeal that knows no change.

And the following remarks of an English writer upon this feature of the Romish hierarchy are very just: "It is this mysterious and indomitable earnestness of the priesthood, which has resisted the attacks of logic, rhetoric, and piety; of divines, philosophers, and statesmen; of wit, humor, and ridicule; and which in this age of learning and science, commerce and liberty, not only enables it to maintain its ground, but to advance and make conquests. The Church of Rome, which would, in the hands of a lukewarm priesthood, fall by the weight of its own absurdity, or be crushed by the hands of its constant assailants, is still strong in the hearts of its members; each of whom, from the Pope down through all its civil and ecclesiastical gradations to the most insignificant member, is a type of concentrated and glowing zeal."

Can a cold, lukewarm church bear up against such intense earnestness? May we sleep while the enemy is ever busy sowing tares? Is it safe, even in our highly favored country, for Christians to fold their arms in listless security, and trust to the intelligence of the people, and the solidity of the civil, political, or religious institutions, as a sufficient guaranty to their liberties? Nay, verily. Not in these, but, under God, in their own ardent and unremitted exertion, must they trust, or else be prepared to suffer a terrible defeat.

Besides the evil influences already referred to, against which the church is called to contend, there is a tendency on its own part, — from which it has even more to fear, — a tendency to accept, and rest satisfied in, a superficial, dead, formal religion.

The great ecclesiastical contest of the world has ever been between spirituality and formalism, — between a simple, free, active religion, on the one hand, and a ceremonious, bigoted, inoperative religion on the other. The latter has often proved too powerful for the former; as is seen in the degeneracy of the Jewish religion, at first comparatively pure, but finally a mere routine of dry and tedious formalities. The same is true of the religion of those lands where the gospel was originally promulgated. At first it triumphed over idolatry with its abominations, and all other untoward influences, and wrought the most wonderful changes in the aspect of society; but finally was displaced by a religion of forms, which under the name of Christianity festered with rank corruption. Look, too, at the lands where Luther, and Calvin, and Zuingle wrought their mighty achievements for God and the truth. A pure faith gained the ascendency, and the reformed churches sprung up in every direction. But in less than fifty years from the time of Luther, most of the churches in Germany had become cold and dead.

And this degenerate tendency is, to-day, as strong as ever before. It is, alas, but too apparent in the present condition of many churches even in our very midst. But is there any necessity for this decline? Is there any immutable law by which this fearful process must go forward? It were a most serious reflection upon the great Author of Christianity, to entertain for a moment a supposition like this.

Where lies, then, the preventive? How shall the church, under God, preserve itself from defection? The question is one of momentous importance, but, nevertheless, easily answered. It is *by being aggressive and diffusive.* Here, as everywhere, the unalterable condition of soundness and health is *energetic activity.*. Hence it is that the early churches maintained their purity and their primitive power, just so long as they pressed their bloodless conquests, and addressed themselves in godliness and sincerity to the work of the Lord. When they became 'strong, and had need of nothing,' as they vainly imagined,—when they were satisfied with present attainments, and were ready to settle down in quiet enjoyment,—just at that point they became lukewarm, and the Saviour was ready to spue them out of his mouth. Sensible of their powerlessness, the next step was to seek aid in State support, and therefore they gladly allied themselves to worldly governments, by the overlaying of which the little life that remained was soon quite smothered to death. "The simple rites of primitive times," as we are told, "were amplified and adorned, and the holy and self-denying spirit of apostles and martyrs took its flight. Christianity ascended the throne of the Cæsars, clothed herself in barbaric splendor, fared sumptuously every day, and became a proud, bloated carcass, splendid to the eye of men, but corrupt and offensive to the eye of God. Antichrist arose; and then formalism and bigotry were enthroned in the professed church of Jesus Christ."

What a lesson does this brief history of bygone days read to the living gospel churches of our day! Does it not say to them in tones of profound emphasis: "Rest not satisfied with present attainments! Beware of indolence and inactivity! If you would enjoy the vigor and freshness and enthusiasm of youth,—if you would maintain the purity and simplicity of the first love,—if you would meet the demands of God and of the age, become not proud of success! Cease not your earnest efforts!

Rest not from your self-sacrificing toils! You must conquer, or be conquered! Either exist aggressively, or not exist at all!

O that these admonitions might be heeded! Already has the process of deterioration far too generally commenced. Already are too many churches slumbering in supposed security. Already are too many Christians "at ease in Zion." Already are they comparatively powerless from inaction.

When evils so great are threatening the welfare of the Church of the living God, — when so many nations are crying for the bread of life, — when so much work needs to be done in our own homes, and congregations, and communities, — and when life's golden moments are so few, ought not every one of us to chide himself for his listless inactivity; and cry, —

> "Up, up, my soul, and on, —
> Thou may'st not linger here,
> Nor toil nor conflict shun,
> Though hedged about with fear.
> Thine be the care
> Each duty to fulfil, each burden share;
> Up, for the coming of the Lord is near!"

Fellow disciple, how much of this earnestness in Christ's service do you possess? If a neighbor of yours were drowning in your sight, and crying out for help, how intent would be your efforts for his rescue! If you were passing a burning house, whose occupants were looking from the windows, and imploring you to furnish them with the means of escape, — how earnestly would you struggle for their deliverance! Should you be less earnest in saving the *souls* of your fellow men from everlasting burnings? O, do you believe what you profess to believe? Do you believe in a judgment, a heaven, and a hell? Do you believe that poor sinners are every moment liable to fall into endless perdition? Then why are you so unconcerned and so inactive with reference to their salvation? Is it strange that ungodly men, unable to reconcile this indifference with your profession, become sceptical of the whole matter of religion?

"Why, Sir," said an infidel to the Rev. Dr. Philip, of Scotland, before he entered upon his mission in Southern Europe, "did I believe as you profess to do, and did I act as you act, I should feel ashamed. You profess to believe that the world is lost, and going to final perdition, and that you have a remedy that can save it:—Why do you not go forth, and plead with your perishing fellow men, with all the earnestness which such a case demands? Why do you not go among the nations that are sitting in darkness, that know not the God of your Bible; and afford them at least a chance of obtaining salvation? If *your* creed were *mine*, I could not rest, till I had warned men of their condition, and entreated them to flee from the wrath to come." O when shall there be no longer occasion for rebukes like this!

Paul was charged with being *beside himself*, when his mind dwelt upon the great things of the kingdom. But upon matters of such pressing moment, the highest enthusiasm is only sober earnestness.

Rowland Hill, once meeting the charge of being an enthusiast, said, "When I first came into this part of the country, I was walking on yonder hill;

and I saw a gravel pit fall in and bury three human beings alive. I lifted up my voice for help so loud, that I was heard in the town below, a distance of a mile, — no one called me an enthusiast then. And when I see eternal destruction ready to fall upon poor sinners, and about to entomb them in an eternal mass of woe, and call on them to escape by repenting and fleeing to Christ, shall I be called an enthusiast? No, sinner, I am not an enthusiast in so doing."

Would to God that every minister, by abandoning the idea of converting men by means of "elegant formalities and poetic appeals," and irresolute, half determined efforts, and by going about the work in downright earnestness, would render himself liable to the same charge! Would to God that all classes of Christians were in this sense enthusiasts! Why should they *not* be in earnest? Christ is in earnest inviting the troubled spirit to come and find rest. God is in earnest calling on sinners to turn and live. Heaven is in earnest, the angels rejoicing over one repenting soul. And hell is in earnest, moving itself for the destruction of those whom you may save from the jaws of death.

Why, then, are *you* inactive? Is it not high time to awake out of sleep? "O my soul," exclaims one, "how much blood, how much weeping, wailing, and gnashing of teeth, will stand to thy account in the day of judgment!" How much will stand to *your* account? Have not souls been already lost through your neglect? Shall others be lost with no prayer, or almsgiving, or effort on your part, for their salvation? See! how they hang, suspended as by a brittle thread, over the burning lake! A single blast, and they fall to rise no more! *Haste*, and throw thine arms around them, and *bring them to Jesus!*

"WAKE, thou that sleepest in enchanted bowers,
Lest these lost years should haunt thee in the night,
When death is waiting for thy numbered hours
To take their swift and everlasting flight;
WAKE, ere the earth-born charm unnerve thee quite,
And be thy thoughts to work divine addressed:
Do something, — do it soon, — with all thy might;
An angel's wing would droop if long at rest,
And God himself, *inactive, were no longer blest.*"

CHAPTER VII.

SIXTH GRAND DEFECT. — WANT OF INDIVIDUALISM.

The most important Thought. — Each for Himself. — No serving God by Proxy. — The Great Commission. — How interpreted by the first Converts. — The Church pure so long as Individualism was recognized. — The Germ of Popery. — Decline and Rise of Individualism. — The Principle not yet practically adopted. — Need of a second Reformation. — Masses unrenewed. — Want of Maturity in Christians. — Want of holy Joy. — Few Additions to Churches. — Slumbering Energies and buried Talents. — A grand Device of Satan to crush Individualism under ponderous Organisms. — Error as to Relation of Ministers and Laymen. — Successful Pastors aided by private Members. — Where lies the Strength of Spiritual Army. — Necessity of Individualism in large Cities. — Lay Agency too much lost sight of. — Oncken and the German Churches. — Lay Missionaries. — Consequences of coming Activity. — Upon Christian Character and Enjoyment. — Upon Spread of Gospel and the Conversion of the World. — Responsibility of Ministers as to its Increase. — Home Thoughts.

It is said that the late distinguished statesman, Daniel Webster, was once asked, "What is the most important thought that ever occupied your mind?" and that he replied, with the deepest seriousness, "The most important thought that ever occupied my mind, was the thought of *my individual responsibility to God.*"

Every man, singly and for himself, is held accountable to God. He is a distinct being. Born apart, apart he dies, and he stands apart at the judgment-seat of Christ.

> "Each, as if he *alone* were there,
> Stood up and won or lost his soul."

And so of every thing pertaining to religion. A man's acts are reckoned as his own, though he were influenced never so much in their performance by others. His *duties* may not be laid over upon another; nor can there be a transfer of conscience. Between his own spirit and his God, no one may interpose, no one can assume responsibility. He is to repent for *himself*, believe for *himself*, live for *himself*, and finally for *himself* stand or fall.

It is precisely in this light that Christianity contemplates man. It views him in his individual capacity. The gospel comes to one alone, and saves that single man, and holds him responsible for certain duties. It converts the individual. Other religions seek to convert men by *masses*. Resort is had to the edict, and the sword, that as nations they may at once submit. But the religion of Christ converts men one by one, — sanctifying a single heart, reforming a single life, elevating a single character, — and thus operates upward and outward through the mass of humanity; just as the particle of leaven, to which it is likened, operates upon the particle lying next to itself, and *it* upon another, until the whole lump is leavened.

Each individual has assigned to him of God, a given position and specific duties. The church of Christ contains within itself a post for every man, which he has no right to abandon. There is no provision made for idlers. The men of wealth may not 'buy off their personal services by the bribe of large donations,' nor may the indigent or "men of low estate," because of the "one talent," refuse to occupy till the Lord shall come. There is no provision by which a man may depute another to serve God *for* him, and thus be released from personal duties. He might as soon pray by proxy, and delegate to another the act of repentance. He is to be himself a discipler, and with his own body and spirit glorify God.

Such is the *individualism* which constitutes a fixed principle in Christ's kingdom. It is known to be such from the Scriptures of divine truth, the only standard of appeal. There the accountability of the individual is everywhere recognized.

Let us view it as related to Christian effort for the salvation of sinners. It is observable in the great commission of our ascended Lord: "Go ye into all the world, and preach the gospel to every creature," (Mark 16: 15); or, as recorded by Matthew, "Go ye, therefore, and teach all nations, — and, lo, I am with you always, even unto the end of the world," (Matt. 28: 19).

In substance this commission is the same, though in form it differs; and it binds every follower of Christ to the work of evangelization. Upon a superficial examination of the circumstances under which it was given, it might appear to have been restricted to the chosen apostles. Indeed, by some, it is so considered; but without foundation. It is true, that in the instance referred to by Mark, it was given to "*the eleven;*" but it is also highly probable, if not absolutely certain, that on another occasion, it was given to the disciples as such.*

It may be added, however, that the commission should by no means be viewed or restricted to the apostles, even on the supposition that it was given to them alone; for many of our Lord's instructions, such as those delivered at the last supper, for example, were given to them alone, but are universally considered as of general application. We may therefore justly conclude that the command to go and teach, — to *disciple* men, — was addressed to no set of men exclusively, but to *believers as such;* to the individuals who loved their Lord then present, and to an equal extent, to *every* follower of Christ in all time.

Hence it was that all of the immediate converts to the true faith, did go forth spreading the news of the great salvation. They, surely, were prepared to interpret the true bearings of the commission; and, acting under it, as soon as they were converted, they began to preach the gospel to others. "At that time there was a great persecution against the church that was at Jerusalem, and they were scattered abroad throughout all the regions of Judea and Samaria, except the apostles." And we are then told that, "Therefore they that were scattered abroad, went everywhere preaching the word," (Acts 8: 1, 4). It is further stated in the Acts of the Apostles, that "they that were scattered abroad upon the persecu-

* See an able discussion of this subject in Notes to Harmony of Gospels, by Dr. Edward Robinson. Part IX.

tion that arose about Stephen, travelled as far as Phenice and Cyprus and Antioch, "preaching the word to none but Jews only." Men of Cyprus and Cyrene, are also mentioned as "preaching the Lord Jesus," though they were neither apostles nor original disciples. And to just such preaching, is to be ascribed the founding of many of the early churches.

But besides these Scriptures, which so distinctly bring to view individual obligation in the work of the gospel, notice our Saviour's intercessory prayer: in which he not only supplicates favors for those who then loved him, but also for those who should "believe through their word;" assuming that they, severally, were to make known to others the way of life eternal.

And again; when long after this the Saviour made, through the beloved disciple, a revelation of things to come, what importance is assigned to this feature of his holy religion! "The Spirit and the bride say, Come: and let him that heareth say, Come!" Let *him* say, let *each one*, personally, take up, and send along down, through all time, the blessed invitation to "Come," and "take the water of life freely."

And is it not interesting to observe that the fullest and sweetest promises and rewards for Christian faithfulness are given as if intended to encourage this individual activity? It is not said the *church* that "converteth a sinner from the error of his ways," but "*he* that converteth" him, shall hide a multitude of sins, and save a soul from death. Nor is it written, the *company*, but "*he* that goeth forth weeping, bearing precious seed, shall doubtless return bringing *his* sheaves with him." Nor will it be said, in the last day, "Well done thou good and faithful" congregation, but "well done thou good and faithful servant, — enter thou into the joy of the Lord." Is there anywhere bestowed upon any company of persons, a commendation equal to that awarded to a single individual, and that individual, too, a *woman?* "*She hath done what she could.*"

Luther used to thank God for those little words, my, thee, thou, thy, me, which are so profusely scattered through the Scriptures, — "The Lord is *my* rock," "*my* fortress," "*my* deliverer;" "When *thou* passest through the waters, I will be with *thee;*" "I will be *thy* God;" "Thou shalt guide *me* by thy counsel, and afterward receive *me* to glory;" — and they only show how *personal* are the blessings and duties of the great salvation.

Moreover, it will be well to notice the expressive language of Christ, as applied to his followers: "Ye are the salt of the earth." From the very figure, their conservative influence is not to be exerted in the form of large, compact bodies, so much as in the capacity of individuals; spread, like grains of salt, all over and throughout society, each loaded with heavenly grace, and contributing his part toward preserving the world from moral corruption. All this is in beautiful harmony with a feature of the divine economy before referred to, — the plan of increasing the ranks of our heavenly King. "Ye shall be gathered one by one, O ye children of Israel," says God. And so it has always been. Christ did not count his converts by thousands, as some one has admirably remarked, nor by hundreds, nor yet by tens; but he counted them by units, saying, "There is joy in the presence of the angels of God over *one* sinner that repenteth." How reasonable, that as results are to be personal and distinct, the operating causes should be so likewise.

Now let it be carefully observed, that, as long as this principle obtained in the early church, — as long as there was kept alive a sense of individual responsibility, and religion was considered to be a personal matter, or, in the affecting language of one of the Platonists, "*The flight of one alone to the only One*," and as long as it manifested itself in individual activity, — so long was the church characterized for its purity and prosperity. But just in proportion as the opposite principle gained the ascendency, and the individual became absorbed in the community, the private member into the official, and men began to serve God by proxy, just in that proportion the church became powerless and corrupt.

A learned writer remarks, that if he were asked, "to what it is owing, chiefly, that the early triumphs of the gospel were arrested,—how it was that Christian usefulness died out of the world, and piety out of the church," — he would suggest that it was to be ascribed "principally to that master device of Satan by which the Christian professor was led to suppose that he could do every thing by proxy; that there was an order of men, on whom, for a certain consideration, he could devolve his duties both to God and man." Who needs to be told that this is nothing more nor less than the germ of popery?—that thus early, and in precisely this way, "the mystery of iniquity" began to develop itself.

What is the essence of popery but 'finding a price for every duty, and discharging from every claim of personal accountableness?' What is the genius of popery but taking away the conscience and the will, and putting the 'judgment and soul under the lock of the confessional, or carrying them about under the frock of a bishop or priest?' What is the system of popery but one vast consolidation, where all power is concentrated into one poor mortal, and the several parts are but cogs and pins performing their functions in absolute subordination to the supreme, central will?

From the fourth to the sixteenth centuries, this gigantic evil overspread most parts of Christendom, and smothered out its religious life. The nominal church was little less than a dead carcass, splendid, indeed, and imposing without, but full of corruption within.

The reign of death was partially interrupted by the Reformation of the sixteenth century. Individual opinion and action became again apparent, and the Christian stood out once more, here and there, as a distinct, responsible agent, accountable to no human being in the concerns of religion, but personally and strictly accountable to God.

Under the preaching of Bunyan and Baxter and Flavel, of the seventeenth century, and of Wesley and Whitefield, Doddridge and Edwards, the Erskines and Tennents, and others of the eighteenth, this tendency toward independent and direct effort on the part of professing Christians was greatly stimulated; and since then, there have been found in the churches not a few who have addressed themselves, in the spirit of primitive times, to the work of the Lord. Their number, however, has not proportionally kept pace with the increase of the avowed disciples of Christ; and *practically* the great principle of individual responsibility for the conversion of souls, remains yet to be generally recognized. *Practically*, there needs to be a *second reformation from popery*. Protestantism itself, in this regard, needs to be reformed.

"It is high time," as has been well remarked, "to inquire, from how much of that enormous system (the papacy) we have been rescued. For just as much of it as still cleaves to us, by just so much are we effectually disabled from doing the first works and emulating the first days of the Christian church." "Now, judging from the past," it is added, "we should say, that the Reformation rescued us from only one half of the evil, — from that part which blinded men to a sense of their personal concern in the affairs of their own salvation. But while the Protestant wonders at the infatuation of the papist in imagining that any thing can exempt him from the necessity of personal diligence in seeking his own salvation, are not we the objects of equal wonder in acting so generally as if we thought any thing could exempt us from the duty of personal activity in seeking the salvation of *others?* If the one is essential popery, equally so, in spirit, is the other also. Glorious, therefore, as the Reformation was for the church, in rescuing its members from the grasp of a spiritual despotism, and making each one feel the necessity of personal faith and personal holiness, as glorious will that reformation be for the world which shall complete the work of deliverance, by rescuing them also from the grasp of selfishness, and making each one feel his own accountability to God for personal activity in the work of human salvation." How surprising that Christians of the United States, who understand so well the essential individualism of *republicanism*, should feel so little the essential individualism of protestantism, — of *Christianity!*

That there *does* exist a lamentable deficiency of this kind of Christian effort, is painfully obvious. Its evidence is furnished in the fact that the masses of men, in immediate proximity to the church of Christ, are still unsanctified and unrenewed. Is there any defect in the glorious gospel of the blessed God? Is not its adaptedness, to the end designed, the same in all ages? Does it not ever remain the wisdom of God, and the power of God unto salvation? Is there any unwillingness, or want of power, on the part of the *Spirit*, whose office work it is to renew the soul? As in his first descent to our guilty world, is he not almighty to save? And if neither in the word nor the Spirit, then is the defect in the *churches.* Their *ministers* are doubtless responsible, in part, for the existing state of things; but in the bosom of the churches themselves lies a principal fault. And that fault is a lack of personal consecration to the one work of leading souls to Christ.

Evidence to the same effect is furnished in the *want of maturity and moral power* in the majority of professors. Every disciple of Christ is required to be in possession of that vigor and manliness of character, that will fit him for enduring hardness as a good soldier of the cross. He is to attain "unto a perfect man; unto the measure of the stature of the fulness of Christ,"—and 'speaking the truth in love, grow up into him in all things which is the head even Christ; from whom the whole body, fitly joined together, and compacted by that which every joint supplieth, according to the effectual working in the measure of every part, maketh increase of the body unto the edifying of itself in love.'

But alas, to how many does the rebuke apply, "When for the time ye ought to be teachers, ye have need that one teach you again,—and are become such as have need of milk, and not of strong meat!" And why this want of a proper and symmetrical development of character,—this well proportioned and thoroughly compacted moral constitution? Is it for want of a sufficient supply of spiritual food, on which they might grow and thrive? So far is this from being the case, that it is to be seriously questioned, whether there is not, in many instances, an *excess* of food administered,—whether the rage for *hearing* sermons does not interfere with their proper digestion; and thus tend to produce feebleness and inefficiency. Does not the language of the apostle, already referred to, indicate the true source of this evil? Is it not because their senses or powers are not "exercised by reason of use,"—because there is not that '*effectual working* of every part that maketh increase in the body?' In both nature and grace, strength and maturity are acquired by one unchanging process—*activity*. Without it the child were always a child. The arm never acquires the bone of iron and the sinew of steel if restrained from use. And so those only who *toil* in Christ's vineyard,—

who abound "in the work of the Lord," — become strong men, "perfect and entire, wanting nothing." There are so many *weak* Christians because there are so few *working* Christians.

And again, do not the frequent complaints that are heard of a want of spiritual enjoyment, evince a general absence of active effort in the Master's service? Have we reason to believe that such complaints were common among the early disciples? And can it be that our Father on high has instituted no means by which we may be continually happy, when at the same time he has taught us to "be glad" in him, to "rejoice in the Lord alway," and that the 'peace of God which passeth all understanding shall keep our hearts?' Why, then, do the children of the King go mourning all their days? Is it not chiefly owing to their inactivity? Shall not the willing and the obedient eat the good of the land? If we feed others, shall not we be fed? Is not happiness always the result of the right action of the moral powers? If there is faithful well-doing, will there not certainly be holy enjoying? Since, therefore, it is proverbially true of Christians in our day, that they do not generally experience that perpetual flow of sweet enjoyment which was apparently possessed by those of apostolic times, is it not evident that they come far short in active engagedness in advancing the Redeemer's cause among men?

And then observe, as another evidence of a sad defect in personal Christian effort, the few additions which are made to the churches, by conversion, from year to year. It has been stated that each missionary of the American Board has been the means of the conversion, on an average, of between three and four hundred souls. And we can readily conceive that, if half the number of professing Christians in the United States were transferred to heathen nations for the purpose of their conversion, we should expect that they would very speedily be the means of converting the whole world to Christ.

But why should so much more be expected of Christians in India or China than in the United States? Are those who go far hence to the gentiles, under any more sacred obligations to put forth earnest efforts to save souls, than are those who remain at home? And is the salvation of an ignorant and degraded heathen a matter of less difficulty than that of an enlightened neighbor, who stands in the same need of being led to Christ? Why, then, do no more conversions occur? Why do large churches, for many years together, receive almost no accessions from the ranks of the enemy? Why are there hundreds and thousands of Christians who have yet to become the direct instrumentality in the conversion of the *first* soul?

There can be but one response to interrogatories like these. It is owing to a culpable neglect of the duty of engaging personally in direct and persevering endeavors to persuade men to become reconciled to God.

These are but a few of the many painful evidences of this neglect. Where do we not behold them? From every point of observation the conviction forces itself upon the mind, that the mass of professed Christians are "at ease in Zion." What an immense assemblage of undeveloped resources does the church of Christ present! Who can contemplate it without being impressed with the idea of a *prodigious latent energy*, — *a reserved force*, of whose utmost power it is impossible to form any adequate conception.

It has been estimated by men of intelligent and careful minds, that "not more than *one fifth* of all who bear the name of Protestant Christians, add any thing of *perceptible* importance to the efficiency of the church, in the work of the world's conversion." From the nature of the case there must be somewhat of conjecture in such an estimate; but under the most favorable aspect, how painful is the sight of the slumbering energies and buried talents in all our churches!

Where are the pious lawyers, physicians, merchants, mechanics, farmers, and statesmen, who daily, hourly watch for opportunities of doing something for Christ? True, here and there one of this character appears, and we have a Williams, Page, Cranfield, Mary Lyon. But the very *prominence* of such individuals is proof of the inactivity of those around them. How many pastors mourn over the want of that coöperation which they *might* enjoy! How many irreligious men and neighborhoods need the pious efforts which might be bestowed!

Societies are too often looked upon as substitutes for personal labors. It has been remarked that no illusion is more common, both in civil and sacred things, than for membership to weaken the sense of responsibility, and even to cause an oblivion of individuality. But, was it the design of Christ that the church should absorb the individual? For what are any combinations formed? Not to neutralize the personal element, but to render it more effective. Does not the efficiency of the whole body depend upon that of its several parts? Men talk of the religion of the church, and the duty of the church; but what is this, if used intelligently, but speaking of the piety and obligations of the individual members of which the church is composed?

And yet under this very illusion, that the church has some responsibility, separate from that of its individual parts, many excuse themselves from personal labor. This is one of Satan's deep devices. For, let it not be forgotten, the adversary of God and man is still plying his devices for the overthrow of Christ's kingdom. Instead of abating his efforts, they are more artful and persistent, as he knows his time is short, and not seldom as an angel of light Alas, that he should succeed so well as to blind the eyes of men to the very fact of his existence; and induce, even in Christians, a forgetfulness, if not a distrust of the fearful truth that as "a roaring lion," he walketh about "seeking whom he may devour!" Did he so beset the Master, — and will he deal gently with the servants? Did he succeed so fearfully in the revolt of the angels, and in the fall in Eden, — and has he become harmless now? It is at our peril that we believe it! And of all his devices no one is more artfully planned, and more widely successful, than that of *crushing individualism under some ponderous organism.* Little does he care how much we make of the *church*, only so the *individual* is lost sight of, and left inactive. It is distinct, direct, and diligent effort on the part of men and women who are zealous for Christ, that gives him most concern.

Besides this practical error in reference to church-membership, there is one equally prevalent and pernicious, as regards the relation of ministers and private members in the work of the gospel. The error consists in looking upon ministers as principally, if not exclusively, intrusted with the concerns of religion. Under the old, preparatory dispensation of Christianity, this was truly the case. Here, a ceremonial holiness and exclusiveness belonged to the official persons; and it was "profanation for any mortal, save the anointed son of Levi, to touch the vessels of the local worship." In the Romish creed, too, and in those which are patterned after it, the clergy are a class above and aside from all other men. To their medium of conveyance is restricted the communication of all grace. According to this theory, God bestows the Spirit through sacramental channels, and has placed in priestly hands "the exclusive patent for saving souls."

Now, while in theory all evangelical Christians pronounce this a gross impertinence, and a most dangerous error, is it not by many practically entertained, only in a modified form? Perhaps unconsciously, but nevertheless in fact, they look upon the propagation of religion as a professional matter, with which they have little or nothing to do. The language of their heart is, Let the men who are ordained to preach, and administer the sacraments of the Lord's house, and attend to the affairs of religion, fulfil the duties of their office. I will be a faithful recipient of the word, and give of my substance to provide for its ministration; and that is as far as *my* duty extends in the matter of gathering souls to Christ. The rest the ministers will attend to: that is their business.

Can any one pretend to justify this from the Scriptures? Can any one assign a reason for believing that he is not under as real an obligation to plan and conduct the affairs of life with direct reference to the promotion of religion, as is any preacher? It may be alleged that preaching is God's chief instrumentality in saving souls. And this is true; but *what kind* of preaching, and *by whom?* Is it not, as some one has in substance observed, the preaching of Philip in the chariot, as well as of Peter to the assembled thousands? — the preaching of the dispersed disciples, as well as of the seventy? — the preaching of the way-side and the fireside, as well as the preaching in the great congregation? — the preaching of Dorcas, and Phebe, and Mary, and Priscilla, as well as of the chosen apostle to the gentiles?

There are many ways of preaching Christ without choosing a text, and standing in a pulpit; and it is not so much of pulpit as of *pew* preaching, that the world has need at the present time. Many ministers of great eminence for their success in promoting the conversion of men, have been largely indebted to this outside preaching of their private brethren. To this, Wesley owed his success in no small degree.

"He encouraged the labors of the pious in every direction, . . . and by this means, under the divine blessing, he increased his own usefulness a thousand-fold; and instead of operating individually, . . . he became the director of a vast system, which remained at work in his personal absence, and was continually pouring into the church its contributions of conquest from the world." Richard Baxter is another example. The wonderful change that occurred in that once wicked field of his labors (Kidderminster), was not produced by his preaching alone. Himself and the converts already gained, made thorough work in visiting, like Paul, from house to house, and addressing individuals and families upon the subject of their soul's salvation. Without ready and active brethren to second his endeavors, the strongest minister is weak, and with them, the weakest is strong.

The church is God's spiritual army, and his ministers are to marshal the hosts "against the mighty." "But what are generals without the rank and file? Success depends scarcely less upon the valor of the individual soldiers, than upon the wisdom of the officers. The conqueror of the world caused to be inscribed upon the spoils taken on one occasion from the enemy, "*Alexander, son of Philip,* WITH THE GREEKS, (*the Lacedæmonians excepted,*) *gained these spoils from the barbarians who inhabit Asia.*" His army, we are told by the historian, were "all brave men," each of them "in case of necessity capable of commanding." It was not Napoleon and his aids alone that won the day in his great battles; but the well-drilled regiments,—the "heavy battalions." And so in things spiritual. If the enemy is to be routed, it is not only needful that there be zeal and prudence in the leaders, but there must be valiant *men*, standing round about them, each one feeling and acting as though the victory depended, under God, upon the weight of *his single arm.*

We have an evil to contend with, 'so gigantic in its strength, so diffused in its influence on all sides of us, and so infectious and malignant in its efforts, that nothing short of the engagement, the energies, and the earnestness, of the whole church can cope with it. The whole church must be employed for the conversion of the whole country. The levy *en masse* must be called out. The enemy is coming in like a flood; infidelity and immorality are invading us; the tocsin must be rung; the beacon fire must be kindled on every hill of Zion; the sound must float from every tower and every battlement, "To arms, to arms!" and every man that can shoulder a musket or bear a pike must take the field and array himself against the foe. Not a single member of a single church, male or female, old or young, rich or poor, but ought to be engaged in personal exertion.'

The necessity of *supplying* the defect which we have now seen to exist, demands attention for a moment more. Take an intelligent view of our large cities. Those great centres of wealth and influence, powerfully affect, either for good or evil, the whole country. The population of the city of New York is estimated at upwards of six hundred thousand. Now for this population there are but about three hundred evangelical preachers, whose time is given exclusively to the ministry. This would give to each minister the care of two thousand souls. And what man is able to do any thing like justice to so numerous a charge, especially with the crushing responsibilities and constant interruptions incident to a city pastorate? Even if they all were attendants, each Sabbath, upon the public services, it were insufficient to meet their spiritual necessities. But it is stated, as we have previously seen,* that one third of this population is not accessible to the ordinary ministrations of the clergy. Now how shall these two hundred thousand persons be operated upon? How shall they be reached? It is simply preposterous to suppose that it can be accomplished by the regularly ordained ministers. Mr. Mann, who has had in charge the religious department of the census of Great Britain, insists that an adequate clerical force cannot be maintained for the large cities. The simple truth is, no clerical force *can* be adequate; for, not to dwell upon the fact that a large proportion of those who never frequent the sanctuary, are opposed to every thing religious, and bitterly prejudiced against the clergy, — which virtually precludes their approaching them even, — let it be borne in mind that during the entire day most of these people are busily engaged in their respective employments, — some in the counting-houses, some in the shops and manufactories, some on the wharves, some in the streets, — and are, therefore, rarely found at home, (if indeed they have any,) or found anywhere, under such circumstances as to render it possible for a

* Chapter I. p. 23.

stranger to approach them, and enter upon profitable religious conversation.

We say again, it is in vain to look to any regularly ordained ministry as adequate to meet this necessity. Nor was it ever *designed* to be met in this way. God never intended that the ministry should do all the work of the churches. There can be *no* condition of society where they will be sufficient to perform it. Nor will the building of more church edifices meet the difficulty, for most of these people do not feel the need of religious instruction, and therefore would not avail themselves of such accommodations.

If this class of the population is to be religiously influenced, it must be, principally, by *lay agency*. Through this means it can be influenced, and that powerfully. Let the lay members of the churches avail themselves of the favorable opportunities which Sabbaths afford for reaching these persons; and go out to meet them in the public grounds, at the corners of the streets, and in their houses. Let them gather the children into Sunday Schools, and the parents into small congregations wherever a few could be collected; let them there, and more privately, converse with them kindly upon the things of religion, and talk to them of a blessed Jesus, and a glorious heaven, giving them the tract and the Bible, and following them with their prayers, and they would bring to bear an untold influence for good.

Take another view of the case. Suppose that each professing Christian were on the watch for a favorable moment to drop a word for Christ, during the weekday employments. Suppose that after his morning prayers in the closet and at the family altar, he were to go forth, with a heart full of love, hoping and praying that he might bless some poor soul before the setting sun. O, who could estimate the moral power of a few thousands of such Christians upon the masses of unconverted men?

Perhaps there is scarcely an individual in that neglected portion of the community alluded to, who does not come into contact with a disciple of Christ almost daily. Thousands of them are in the employ of pious builders, and merchants, and manufacturers, whose advantages and responsibilities for doing them good are every way important. Many of them have pious shop mates and companions; and all, more or less frequently, meet and mingle with those who bear the Christian name. What opportunities, then, have pious laymen for impressing with the truths of religion the minds of those whom ministers cannot reach!

The truth is, lay-agency has been too much lost sight of. Altogether too little is said and written concerning it. It is an omen for good, that it is beginning to attract attention. The English statistician, above alluded to, particularly mentions the fact that the Wesleyans of England have "twenty thousand preachers and class-leaders, not belonging to the ministerial order." Many have witnessed with surprise, the statements that are made of the wonderful success of the gospel in connection with the labors of Mr. Oncken in Germany.

Twenty years ago, in the city of Hamburg, a band of seven brethren assembled in a shoemaker's shop, laid their hearts together upon the altar of God's service, and formed themselves into a church, of which Mr. Oncken was chosen pastor. Now behold the results! The little church of seven members has multiplied itself into fifty churches! Ten thousand souls have been hopefully converted; fifty millions of persons have heard the true gospel; and eight millions of pages of tracts, and four hundred thousand copies of the Scriptures have been put into circulation.

How has this work, under God, been accomplished? Let us learn from the pastor's own lips: "All our members were initiated and instructed into a regular system of operations. *Every man and woman* is required to do something for the Lord, and thus the Word of the Lord has been scattered. We have now about seventy brethren in Hamburg, who go out *every alternate Sabbath*, two by two, preaching the gospel; and by this means the whole of the city has heard the precious name of Christ." "We think that all the talents in the church should be brought out. A list of the brethren who can speak is kept, and they are sent to villages to preach on the Sabbath, and they go out as the church directs. Then apart from these laborers and from the labors of the female members, we have an interesting machinery which has worked well, and costs nothing,—and that is the travelling apprentices. It is the custom of apprentices to travel after learning their trades, and many come to Hamburg. They are supplied with tracts, which they distribute at home and abroad. In Vienna and in Pesth, thousands of tracts and Bibles were scattered during the revolution, the way for which had been prepared by these young men." It is stated that there is scarcely a female member of the large church in Hamburg, who has not two or three Bibles and a parcel of tracts to distribute; and that, in a single year, through the six hundred members of the church and its pastor, every family in that city of one hundred and fifty thousand inhabitants, was visited, for the purpose of religious conversation, and the distribution of books. And there is this remarkable circumstance beside; that though these devoted men and their brethren in other parts of Germany, form less than fifty churches, they keep up preaching at nearly four hundred stations!

When all these facts are taken into the account, need we marvel at their success? God's plans of operation are all perfect. We have but to follow them, and we shall surely witness, as in this instance, the most happy results.

Some of the foregoing remarks, as to the necessity of the coöperation of the private members of the churches with the minister, are specially applicable to cities; but the call for such coöperation is confined to no particular localities or conditions of society. How few are the places where brethren might not be profitably employed, like the Germans referred to, in the capacity of *lay*-preachers, a class of laborers once so effective. Men there are, in most of the churches, of ardent piety, and of sufficient ability to interest and instruct an audience, but whose gift for exhortation is rarely exercised. There is more of this talent than is generally supposed; and by cultivation, it would be still more generally possessed.

And why should these gifts be suffered to lie idle? Has God given to men any talents which he does not design to be improved? And have the churches any right to suffer such gifts to remain unoccupied, yielding no returns to him who bestowed them with the command, "Occupy till I come?" Especially is it requisite that they render available such talent at a time like the present, when the demand for laborers in the ministry is so much greater than the supply. Where is the congregation that might not sustain an out station to advantage, if it were in the power of the minister to assume the additional labor? In most cases it is beyond his power; and hence preaching stations, and in many instances feeble churches, are left destitute. But if these lay-brethren are sought out, and encouraged to engage in the work, the necessity is met, to some extent, at least. If they can interest their brethren in the social meeting, why not an equally large gathering in some destitute neighborhood? If they are listened to with interest when they speak to their fellow-citizens upon subjects of a civil or political nature, why may they not address them, with equal propriety and acceptableness, upon the great concerns of religion?

Moreover, the time will come, when lay-missionaries will be universally considered as indispensable in the work of evangelizing the heathen. Already has it been said in the high places of Zion, "It may be well to institute the inquiry, whether among the means and methods of evangelizing the heathen, it should not be projected by laymen, of all arts and professions, we do not say to be sent, but to send themselves, in the arrangements of their own trade, toil, and traffic, all over the earth, for the express purpose of being succorers of the gospel, rearing churches, ... in their own homes, and pouring light and love through all the channels of secular intercourse, upon the souls of the benighted." * And no one can read the chapter on "Laymen called to the Field of Missions," from the glowing pen of the lamented Dibble, without being impressed with the conviction, that in this department of effort, laymen have yet to perform an important part.† And so in other departments of Christian activity. The distinction between the ministry and the membership of the churches, as regards the obligation to diffuse the gospel, is far too sharply defined. The work of the churches is far too generally given over into the hands of the officials. How different from the time when those unordained ministers went out from Jerusalem, *preaching everywhere the word!*

When primitive piety shall once more prevail, how marked, and how pleasing shall be the change! Then no professor, lay or clerical, will desire exemption from this responsibility and labor. Then, like Simon and Philip, will converted men say, "We have found the Messiah," and like him from whom the evil spirit was cast out, 'go home to their friends, and tell how great things the Lord hath done for them.' Then shall the preachers of the gospel

---

* Rev. Dr. Adams's Sermon before the American Board of Commissioners for Foreign Missions, preached at Cincinnati, Ohio, Oct. 4, 1853.

† See Thoughts on Missions, by Rev. Sheldon Dibble, pp. 111–134.

send to other churches, as of old, the salutations of their "fellow-workers unto the kingdom of God, which have been a comfort unto them," and tell, with grateful emotions, of an Apelles, and Aquila, and Epenetus; a Lucius, a Rufus, and a Nereius; and of Marys and Priscillas; of Persis and Tryphena and Tryphosa, and "those women which labored with" them "in the gospel;" and of others, their "fellow-laborers, whose names are in the book of life." And then shall hosts of men and women be found, consecrated, in the highest sense, to God's service; — "deacons and deaconesses, brothers and sisters of charity, filled with Christ's love in their hearts, — priests and priestesses, self-devoted to the high-priest's own work of going about to do good."

The happy results of such universal activity, who can fully appreciate? How blessed in its influence, both upon unconverted men, and individual Christian character! Personal piety will thereby be greatly promoted; for, by no other method is it so effectually advanced, as by thinking, and praying, and acting, for the eternal salvation of those perishing in sin. Christians will then possess a breadth, and depth, and strength of character — a manliness and maturity — now seldom witnessed. They will become *healthful*, *energetic*, *animated* followers of Christ. The "weak in Zion" will become "as David; and the house of David as the angel of the Lord."

Then will there be more of constant rejoicing in the Lord. "O, there is a richness of holy joy," exclaimed a missionary, "in yielding up all to God, and holding ourselves as waiting servants to do his will!" "I love the mission work," said another, "and the cause of Christ, and the children of God, more and more every day; and every night I go to my pillow with a heart, — oh, *so* full and happy!" Howard's prescription for a heavy heart, is after the divine order, — "Set about doing good to somebody. Put on your hat and go out and visit the sick and the poor; inquire into their wants, and administer unto them; seek out the desolate and oppressed, and tell them of the consolations of religion. I have often tried this method, and have always found it the best medicine for a heavy heart." The Spartans had a law that no child should partake of his meal, until sweat was seen to stand on his forehead. Of higher antiquity was that law which reads, "If ye be willing and obedient, ye shall eat the good of the land." He eats most of Christ's *dainties*, who performs most of Christ's *duties*.

Then how speedily shall the news of the great salvation break upon the ear of every mortal! When the cry of fire is first raised in a populous town, it is echoed back by a single voice. In a moment it is caught up by another, and by another still, and so spreads outward until the alarm becomes universal.

President Wayland's illustration, drawn from the event of the proclamation of peace in New York, at the close of the last war with Great Britain, is exceedingly forcible and appropriate. After describing the gloomy prospects of the nation, he states from personal observation, that on a Saturday afternoon in February, a ship was discovered in the offing, which was supposed to be a cartel, bringing home our commissioners at Ghent, from their mission. The sun had set gloomily before any intelligence from the vessel had reached the city. Expectation became intense as the hours of darkness drew on. At length a boat reached the wharf, announcing the fact that a treaty of peace had been signed. The men on whose ears these words first fell, rushed in breathless haste into the city, to repeat them to their friends, shouting as they ran through the streets, peace! peace! peace! Every one who heard the sound repeated it. The news spread with electric rapidity. The whole city was in commotion. Men bearing lighted torches were flying to and fro, shouting like madmen, peace! peace! peace! Few slept. One idea occupied the mind; and every one becoming a herald, the news soon reached every man, woman, and child in the city. Would the news of "peace on earth," spread with less rapidity through the whole world, were each disciple to thus promptly act *his part* in its promulgation?

And *what power shall attend the messages thus delivered!* It is stated that the mission churches in Burmah have been almost exclusively raised up by means of Zayat preaching; which is little else, for the most part, than sitting down and conversing upon religion with a single individual, or a group of individuals, who may be present. How like Christ's method of making converts! There is power in direct appeal. The fact that the unconverted are so reluctant to put themselves in the way of personal conversation on religious subjects, notwithstanding their readiness to hear preaching in public, is a striking proof of this. So also in the process by which revivals of religion generally progress; which is mainly, or at least to a great extent, through the private and personal efforts of Christians of experience, and of those who are recent converts.

Now suppose that Christians, generally, should adopt this method, and address themselves, in good earnest, to the work of the world's conversion. If they numbered but five hundred thousand upon the whole earth, and each one of them should become the means of converting one soul a year; and if, from year to year, these five hundred thousand persons, and those converted through their instrumentality, should go on, severally leading one soul to Christ yearly, in the short space of *thirteen* years, leaving a wide margin for increase of population and decrease of laborers, the whole world would be converted. But, in fact, instead of five hundred thousand Christians, there are, of those who make what may be termed an intelligent profession of religion in the different parts of the world, perhaps *twelve millions*, or *twenty-five times* the number above supposed. Alas, that such an immense army should make such slow aggressions upon the kingdom of darkness! Alas, that such a prodigious force should be accomplishing so little!

Some one has made the following calculation. Suppose the work of evangelization to be commenced in the ministry of a single believer; and suppose his labors and prayers during one year to result in the conversion of a single individual. Then suppose these two to labor the second year with the same result, each of them being instrumental in the conversion of another, so that a little band of four brethren enter on the third year. Now taking the population of the globe at nine hundred millions, and supposing their agency to advance thus, by geometrical progression, it is easy to tell when they will overtake the whole field. By following out the problem, it will be seen, that long before the first laborer, in the ordinary course of nature, should be gathered to his fathers, there would not be left a single outcast on earth beyond the blessed fraternity of faith and love!

Perhaps the view is more impressive still, if confined to a narrower scale. In the United States, as previously seen, we have one member of some evangelical church, to every seven individuals of the whole population. Now, by deducting the professing Christians, and a suitable number for the infant portion of the community, it will be seen that if every believer were to attempt the conversion, under God, of some five individuals within the space of the next year, and were successful in leading them to a knowledge of the truth, every man, woman, and child within the limits of the whole country might be enrolled as a follower of Christ, by the expiration of that short period of twelve months! And yet, would the immediate conversion of the small number of five individuals, be too much for the humblest disciple to attempt for God, and expect from God?

When, therefore, we look abroad and behold the world lying in wickedness, it must be remembered, that there is a force, every way adequate, through Christ, to its complete and speedy rescue. To bring that force into *action* is all that is required.

Numerous as are the ranks of the unconverted,

they will most surely and most rapidly disappear when once the passion for saving souls takes possession of the individual members of Christ's church on earth, — when, in the warehouse and in the shop, in the factory and in the mill, in the granary and in the field, on the road side and at the fireside, in the city and in the country, on the sea and on the shore, men and women are eagerly watching to proselyte some soul to Christ, — when 'love for the world shall burn in *each* heart, prayer for the world ascend from *each* lip, bounty for the world drop from *each* hand, the message of mercy gush from *every* tongue.' Then, O *then*, shall linger no longer the salvation of a ruined race!

For the introduction of such a state of things, the responsibility of *ministers* is great indeed. If it is ever to be brought about, it must be, mainly, through their instrumentality. It seems to be needful, first of all, that questions like these should be more closely studied, and more frequently discussed from the pulpit and platform, and through the public press. What are the mutual relations of ministerial and lay agency, in the work of the gospel? How shall the moral force of the entire membership of the churches be called forth, and brought to bear most effectively upon the advancement of the Redeemer's kingdom? Besides this, it is necessary that pastors give increased attention to the development of the energies of their people; by opening to them avenues of usefulness, and stimulating them, by every possible means, to engage personally in the work of the Lord.

The words of Dr. Harris upon this subject, cannot be too seriously pondered. " The man of God when put in trust with the ministry of a particular church, is to look upon each of its members as a talent, concerning which the divine Proprietor is saying, – 'Occupy till I come, — employ every member, — every moment and faculty of every member, — to the best advantage, that each may be the means of winning another, and that my church of five hundred may be the means of gaining other five hundred more.' With this solemn charge resting on his spirit, he will feel that his first object is to make most of that church, with whose instrumentality his Lord has intrusted him. Its members may not be educated, wealthy, numerous, nor in a worldly sense influential. But they are such as God hath collected and formed into a church to take part in his sublime purpose of saving the world.

"One thing is certain, therefore, that they are all to be employed. In this sense there are to be no 'private Christians' among them. Every believer is a public man, taken up into the universal designs of the God of grace. In whatever sense they are private, then, like the ranks of an army all are to take the field; the only concern of the minister must be how to dispose of his forces so as to render them most effective in the cause of God. A ministry which begins and ends with itself, — however pious, intelligent, and eloquent it may be, — is only the ministry of one man; and even that counteracted, neutralized, and often rendered worse than useless, by the slumbering and selfish inactivity of the people. But a ministry which sets and keeps in motion an entire church, however destitute it may be of other qualifications, becomes, in effect, the ministry of all its members, and thus proves an instrumentality of the widest influence and of the greatest efficiency. And never till the entire church is thus moved, and all its resources put into actual requisition, will the full value of the Christian ministry be seen; for never till then will it fully answer the high object of its divine appointment in the conversion of mankind."

And finally, believer in Christ, whose eye now rests upon this page, are *you* acting a faithful part in the great work of bringing back to Christ an estranged world? Perhaps you are a "private member" only, of the church, and on this account are accustomed to suppress the uprising of an occasional and troublesome sense of neglect of duty, it may be toward a beloved child, or companion, or friend, for whose conversion you have at times felt somewhat concerned. But you are, with great earnestness and affection, entreated to consider well whether God does, or does not accept, the excuses which you are wont to render for such neglect. Will your plea that you lack the means, or the time, or the opportunity, or the gift that is necessary, be acknowledged valid in the judgment? How many are the opportunities of usefulness, if you had but a heart to embrace them? There is the unconverted member of your own household,—there the Sunday school, and the tract district,—there a destitute neighborhood and an afflicted family, and a group of fatherless or motherless children,—there is a dying couch and a disconsolate widow, a burdened inquirer, a thoughtless sinner, a cold backslider,—and where you will you *may* do good. Is it not possible that some unconverted individual is surprised that you do not speak to him as to the interests of his soul? Has not some one, partly through your neglect, been led substantially to say with a certain young man, 'I have always been in the habit of attending church on the Sabbath. For nearly two years I have been constant at a particular meeting, but who of the entire congregation knows whether I am a professor or non-professor? How many of this large congregation have spoken to me upon this subject, or show any desire to know my feelings upon it? Not one. Who cares for me, whether I be eternally saved, or lost?'

Paul anticipated pleasure in meeting those in heaven, whom he had instrumentally saved: "For what is our hope, or joy, or crown of rejoicing? Are not even ye in the presence of the Lord Jesus Christ, at his coming?" Are you willing to go home to heaven with *not one* soul to present to Christ,—not one soul whom you may look upon, through all eternity, as saved in connection with your endeavor? Who would covet the heaven of such an one? Many opportunities you have already suffered to pass by unimproved; but you may yet 'save a soul from death, and hide a multitude of sins.' If you feel the force of no abiding motive, urging you to this duty, go to the cross of Christ, and there study your obligations anew. Consider also how ready is God to bless the humblest efforts of his children. That devoted servant of Christ referred to above, as having done so great a work in Germany, owed his conversion, under God, to an humble individual with whom he resided when a young man in London.

The efforts of a gentleman from Scotland, during a brief residence in Geneva, some forty years since, were a main agency in the conversion of Frederic Monad, and Felix Neff, and the eminent historian of the Reformation, Dr. J. H. Merle D'Aubigne, and several others. Who can gather up the results of those labors for Christ? Baxter's first religious impressions were produced by the personal conversation of his father. Harlan Page, by religious conversation with those with whom he met, by writing letters to unconverted persons, by giving away tracts, and establishing prayer-meetings, and the like means, though by trade a carpenter, accomplished results compared with which those of many a minister even, are trivial. And when this good man was about to die, he could say, "I know it is all of God's grace, and nothing that I have done: but I think that I have had evidence that more than one hundred souls have been converted to God through my own direct and personal instrumentality."

Follow the example of this servant of the Lord, even as he followed Christ. Wait not for opportunities to do some *great* work. Use such as *now* present themselves. Seize every favorable moment to drop a word for your Master, — to impress a soul with saving truth, — to bring back a wanderer to the favor and the fold of God. Do it with a gentle, tender, earnest spirit. Do it with much prayer for success. The carrier-pigeon first flies directly upward, and then outward to its destination. So in your errands of mercy; first mount upward on wings of faith toward heaven, and then haste to do the Master's bidding. And be not weary in well-doing; for, in due season, you shall reap, if you faint not.

CHAPTER VIII.

THE GRAND REMEDY FOR ALL EXISTING DEFECTS IN CHRISTIAN CHARACTER — A GENERAL AND POWERFUL REVIVAL OF RELIGION IN THE CHURCHES.

Recapitulation. — Where the Promise of his Coming? — A powerful and extensive work of Grace the grand Means of Progress. — The Spirit of God the animating Agency in the Church. — Aggressive Movements of Modern Times the fruit of Revivals. — Permanence and Welfare of our Country to be attributed to special Outpourings of the Spirit. — Such Seasons now required. — Need of, in the great Centres of Influence. — In all parts of the Land. — Position of this Country, and sublime Mission of the American Churches. — Revivals gained, all gained. — Pentecostal Scenes to be expected. — Ministers to labor for their Return. — Christians generally to awake and come up to the help of the Lord. — Concluding Appeal.

UPON a review of the preceding pages, it will be seen that we were led, first of all, to inquire into the actual existence of any serious defects in the prevailing piety of the age; and that we were compelled, from various considerations, to adopt the painful conclusion that such defects do really exist. We then proceeded to consider several prominent features of the piety of primitive times, in respect to each of which there is now an alarming deficiency. These were, simplicity of purpose, — consecration to God, — a scriptural faith, — self-denial for Christ, — earnestness, — individualism.

An examination like this, of subjects most intimately related to the welfare of Christ's kingdom on earth, is adapted to awaken emotions of no ordinary character. The thoughtful, praying disciple, whc has long waited for the glorious day predicted of old, will almost involuntarily exclaim: Great God, where is the promise of thy coming? Is this thine earth, — the world pledged to thy Son for a pure inheritance and an undisputed possession? Are not six hundred millions of the race still under the almost entire control of Satan? Does not the destroyer still walk abroad as the god of this world? Does not idolatry still defy the heavens? Alas! Maker of the universe, what a debased and maddened world turns round to thine eye! How long! O how long!

> "For near six thousand years thy foe
> Has triumphed over all below;
> Save that a little flock is found,
> With ravening wolves encompassed round!"

When, *when* shall the reign of the tempter end?

More affecting still, if possible, to the pious soul, is the condition of the church. Amid some things that are encouraging, how much there is to sadden the heart! How much worldliness, and selfishness! How much deadness to spiritual objects! How much insensibility to the perils and woes of dying men! How many unsanctified hands, and hearts, and possessions! And how little of that faith which ventures all on God, and which subordinates this world to the next! How little of suffering and sacrificing for Christ, and of ardent and personal endeavor to save souls from going down to perdition!

And with what emphasis comes the cry of one of Zion's most faithful watchmen: 'O what, and who shall rouse the church of God to a sense of her duty, her destiny, and her honor, as God's instrument for converting an ungodly world? Where is the more than trumpet breath that, with the thunders of the skies, and the voice of eternal truth, shall break in upon the slumber of a luxurious and unbelieving church! What visitations of mercy or of judgment; what internal commotions, or external assaults; what national convulsions or social disruptions, are necessary to arouse her to her work, and prepare her to perform it! When shall every Christian feel that God's chief end in keeping him out of heaven for a season is, that he might keep immortal souls out of hell? When shall another Luther rise up to reform us from our worldliness, even as the first delivered us from Popery? When shall another Whitefield pass through the midst of us, and with his burning eloquence, kindle a fire of zeal in our hearts which shall consume the earthliness, and purify the gold of our faith?'

The means by which the defects that have been particularly considered, are to be removed, and the churches rendered more efficient, is a branch of our subject already partially noticed in the main discussion. It is deserving, however, of special attention. Those means are varied in their character, and in degrees of importance. But there is one remedy excelling, heaven wide, all others; and, indeed, concentrating all others into itself: and that is, a general and powerful revival of pure religion. Nothing short of the indwelling of a larger measure of the divine Spirit, which constitutes a genuine revival, can effect the removal of those alarming evils which afflict the church, and the world. And this can effect their removal. These are the two propositions to be maintained.

Observe, then, that *the Spirit of God is the grand animating agency in the Christian Church.* He first gives life to the soul, and afterward sustains and increases that vital energy. The vigor of the whole spiritual being depends upon his presence. He is the sanctifier of the soul. He enables us to overcome and eradicate the remains of sin within us; and gives to the new nature symmetry, beauty, maturity, and strength. And what he does for an individual Christian, he also accomplishes for the body of believers. When the ark abode in the house of Obed-edom, it was doubly blessed and happy. When God's presence was manifested among his people of old, it diffused bloom and beauty all abroad. 'Carmel's summit displayed a richer green; Hermon's acclivity with its varying belts of cloud and sunshine, sent forth more fertilizing vapor to irrigate the soil; Ophir and Tarshish poured still ampler stores into the marts of trade; health smiled on every hand; and each one sat under his own vine and fig-tree, none daring to molest or make afraid.' And so when God's spiritual garden is favored with the special divine presence, the dry and barren ground is made to abound with springs of water, and become fruitful soil; the drooping vines revive,

"The spices yield their rich perfume;
The lilies grow and thrive."

Who that has witnessed the effects of a powerful revival of religion upon the hearts and lives of God's children, has failed to observe that the eye is then single, the energies and affections are cheerfully consecrated to God, faith is in vigorous exercise, the saving of souls, and the concerns of the world to come, occupy the mind, and this world, as Edwards represents it, speaking of the light in which it was viewed by the people of New England during the great awakening of his time, "is a thing only by the by."

And hence it is that, while under the influence of the Holy Spirit the imperfections of the people of God disappear, their preparedness for the subjugation of a wicked world to Christ, is secured. Then are they possessed, not alone of the principle of *life*, but of *power* also. In the tabernacle service, the sacred utensils, and the priests were of no avail, except the *cloud* appeared, which symbolized the divine presence. And in equipping his servants for their mission, they were directed by the Lord to "tarry at Jerusalem," until they should experience the promised descent of the Holy Spirit. He came, at length, and then were they "endued with power from on high." Then went they forth to subdue the enemies of the cross, and triumphed in all places. So in every advance which the church has made since the days of the apostles. It has not been by might, nor by human power, but by God's Spirit. The measure of the gift of the Spirit has always determined the measure of success. The larger the outpouring from above, the larger the ingathering upon earth.

It is interesting to notice, also, in support of our

position, *the more remarkable aggressive movements of the Christian church in modern times;* and observe how clearly they may be traced to extensive revivals of religion. Not to dwell upon the early efforts of Eliot and the Mayhews to evangelize the American Indians — efforts which had their rise in a revival under the labors of the old Puritans, — nor upon the mission of Swartz and others from Germany to India, which owed its origin to the revival of the Protestant faith under Francke, Spener, and those of kindred spirit, — nor upon the missionary enterprise of the Moravians, which may be traced to the successful labors of Zinzendorf, — let us turn to the great missionary movement of the present century.

We must look for the remote cause of that glorious enterprise, as far back as the period of the "Great Awakening," which dates from about the year 1740. Associated with that wonderful work of grace, is the brilliant constellation of familiar names, — Wesley, Whitefield, Romaine, Wren, Lady Huntington, Doddridge, Erskine, the Tennants, Davies, Brainerd, Edwards. Both in this country and in Great Britain, vital, evangelical religion was extensively revived. Edwards, who has so fully written the history of its rise and progress in the United States, says, "It might be said at that time, in all parts of the country, 'who are these that fly as a cloud and as the doves to their windows?'" In respect to his own field of labor he observes, "There was scarcely a single person in all the town, old or young, left unconcerned about the great things of the eternal world." "The town seemed to be full of the presence of God; it was never so full of love, nor of joy, and yet so full of distress, as it was then." "A loose, careless person, could scarcely be found in the whole neighborhood; and if there *was* any one, it would be spoken of as a strange thing."

The fruits of that work remain unto this day. How largely they entered into the grand, immediate causes of the missionary movement, it is impossible to tell. Doubtless as their result, in part, were Heber and Martyn and Buchanan and Carey sent forth, from the mother country, to preach salvation to the heathen. And, doubtless, as regards our own land, the work of grace at the beginning of the present century, was, in some sense, but the *renewal* of that work which had preceded it.

But coming down to the time last indicated, the year 1800, we meet with one of the most blessed revivals with which the churches have ever been favored. At that time began the moral change, which, as says Dr. Griffin, "swept from so large a part of New England its looseness of doctrine and laxity of discipline, and awakened an evangelical pulse in every vein of the American church." Then it was that the same individual, speaking of certain parts of Connecticut, could make mention of "thrice twenty congregations, in contiguous counties, as laid down in one field of divine wonders." And just here, by this gracious visitation from on high, were quickened into life the germs of those great benevolent institutions, which are the glory of our country and age. The laborers, themselves, in that revival, became missionaries in every direction. One was sent into a destitute part of Vermont; some plead, with trumpet tongue, the cause of missions at home and abroad, and some organized local societies for its promotion.

Here we begin to recognize the name and influence of Samuel J. Mills, who originated in one of the counties where the power of God was remarkably displayed, and from whom the eloquent Griffin, according to his own testimony, received that mighty impulse which enabled him to become so efficient in the formation of several benevolent organizations. Close by the side of young Mills, Gordon Hall originated; who became one of the pioneer missionaries. Connected with another of the godly men who shared a part in that glorious awakening, was James Richards, who was one of the six young men who declared to a meeting of Congregational ministers in Massachusetts, in the year 1810, their intention to preach the gospel to the heathen.

It is to these very three individuals — Mills, Hall, Richards — and with them Judson and Rice, that we refer those prayers and communings, those holy aspirations and high resolves, which invest with such grandeur the commencement of the American missionary enterprise. They are the men concerning whom it is written, that, while students at Williams College, "On Wednesday afternoons they used to retire for prayer to the bottom of the valley south of the west college; and on Saturday afternoons, when they had more leisure, to the more remote meadow on the bank of the Hoosac; and there, under the haystacks, those young Elijahs prayed into existence the embryo of American missions."

But, however important the results of that gracious outpouring of God's spirit in arousing the churches of Christ to systematized and determined efforts for the salvation of the Gentiles, they were scarcely less important upon the permanent welfare of our own country.

At the period to which we refer, the war of the Revolution had just been terminated. During that war many churches had been disorganized; their members had been called to the battle field; the houses of worship had been converted into hospitals; the public mind had been engrossed with other than religious subjects; and vital piety had suffered a decline. Worse than this: the opinions of sceptical French philosophers were becoming prevalent. Sympathizing with France in her struggles, as this nation could not fail to do, it almost naturally imbibed her irreligious principles; and we were fast becoming a nation of infidels. That revival was the lifting up of the standard, when the enemy was coming in like a flood. Then it was that Dr. Dwight and others preached and wrote so powerfully. The Spirit of God came down upon the college of which this good and great man held the presidency, on no less than four special occasions, and more than two hundred young men embraced the gospel, who in their turn were the means of saving thousands of others. In every direction, the "truth as it is in Jesus" triumphed over error. Churches were reorganized, and planted in new localities; the ministers and members grew strong again under the fresh anointing from on high, and "believers were the more added to the Lord, multitudes both of men and women." Then followed the fervent appeals, and wise deliberations, and liberal devisings, in connection with which our various benevolent organizations, of different names and spheres of action, arose.

Such have been some of the results, in times past, of the extensive revival of pure religion. How obvious that it is *precisely this that is now required* for the perfecting of Zion, and the successful prosecution of enterprises which she has so nobly commenced!

That which is needful is, the elevation of the entire church of Christ on earth, to a higher position in point of holiness. Of numbers, and intelligence, and wealth, she is now possessed. There is no element of influence wanting, save that chief, and *only real* element of power, *vital godliness.* Without more of this she cannot long maintain even her present position. She is now but slowly advancing. It is with a halting, trembling step. At times she even seems to falter; and at some points her forces absolutely retreat; while the enemy exultingly cries, Where is now thy God? and threatens to drive her from the field.

What can save our large cities but a powerful revival of religion? In the present state of things, as we have seen in the opening chapter of this work, while the population is rapidly increasing, the churches, as to numbers, are scarcely holding their own. Infidelity, intemperance, licentiousness, — every form of irreligion, and every species of vice, may there be seen springing up, and flourishing in a luxurious growth. And more painful still to contemplate, the churches appear to be departing from the simplicity of the gospel, and, in many instances, by the array of wealth and fashion, and the expense consequent upon it, absolutely placing beyond the reach of the masses, the privileges of God's house. Indeed, partly from this circumstance, and partly from their own indifference to all religious subjects, the great bulk of the lower classes, in many of our cities, is, in no proper sense of the term, operated upon by the religious part of the community. What must be the end of these things, unless some radical change is effected, it is not difficult to foretell. It is written in the epitaphs of those mighty and wicked cities of old, buried, long since, in oblivion. Will any thing short of a powerful work of grace effect the needful change? Will any thing short of this reach and eradicate the fearful evil? Who can devise any other adequate remedy? This, and this alone, is efficacious. It would uproot and overturn the most deep-seated and far-spreading vices, — it would lead to the consecration of the vast treasures of wealth there accumulated, and to a great extent in the hands of professed Christians, — and, by purifying, and filling with new life the great centres of action, it would cause to be sent forth to the furthermost extremities of the land, influences for good.

But why speak we of particular localities? Let any one cast his eye over our broad and beautiful domain, — let him call to mind the origin, the history, and the character of the people who mainly inhabit it, and their commerce, and language, and institutions, — let him consider its geographical position as related to other portions of the globe, — and its moral position as related to the world of corrupt and vitiated civilizations on the one hand, and paganism on the other, — and also the wonderful providences of God, which have, of late, given to us such vast regions of rich territory, at the same time burst open the floodgates for the nations to rush in and possess it, — and he cannot but exclaim, "O for a voice of mighty thunderings to rally the forces of our American Christendom, for another bold, prayerful, self-devoted, *Puritan* effort to found the institutions of the Bible all over these vast plains, and build God's altars all along these mighty streams, before the god of this world shall have here forged his deadly missiles and fortified his strongholds!" A *powerful, wide spread revival* would gain these glorious results.

What *one thing*, therefore, does this whole country so loudly call for, as the *descent of the Holy Ghost upon the churches?* Its salvation must "*come out of Zion.*" If its foundations be not sapped by prevailing immorality, — if it fall not into the hands of Barbarism, nor Anarchism, nor Romanism, — if it be not rent asunder by internal dissensions, — if it call not down upon itself the swift vengeance of God, because of its aggravated national and individual sins, — then it must be because the Most High has here a people who fear him and keep his testimonies, — it must be because they, the salt of the earth, spread abroad throughout the entire mass of society a sanctifying and conservative influence.

And let it remain in every mind, as a deep, inwrought conviction, that *only* by a more general indwelling of the Divine Spirit, can this sublime mission of the American churches be accomplished. They may build houses for worship in every nook and corner of the land, — they may endow hundreds of institutions of learning, — they may perfect their methods and means of doing good, — they may do battle upon the many and complicated vices which afflict humanity, — they may aim at the correction of domestic abuses and political evils, — and in doing it may gain important ends for the cause of righteousness and truth, — but in order to final and complete success, there must be *an increase of the Spirit of the Most High* in the hearts of those who bear the Christian name. Nothing else can make the churches strong. Nothing else can remove the existing defects of piety, and render it efficient. These defects are beyond the reach of all expedients. Their roots run too deep, and are too firmly interwoven with the depravity of our nature, to be eradicated by mere human volition. There must be something that is *elemental* in its operations. Far down in the heart, must be felt the hidden power of Almighty grace, working mightily at the very *fountains* of life and action, and imparting new vigor and force.

This gained, all is gained. There is not a single thing required for carrying forward to ultimate success the work of the Lord, which this indwelling of the divine efficacy would not secure.

Is there a demand for more laborers in the *ministry*, both at home and abroad? Suppose the work of God to be revived in all our colleges and seminaries of learning, would not the demand most certainly be met? One hundred of the converts in nine revivals which occurred in Dartmouth College, are known to have entered the ministry. And who can tell how large has been the accession to the ministerial force, from the numerous revivals with which Yale, Williams, Amherst, Hamilton, Middlebury, and other colleges, have been blessed in years gone by?

Is there a demand for intelligent, active *laymen*, to lead on our noble enterprises? A revival among the young men at their schools of learning, or in the bosom of the churches, would meet the demand. "Every student in a college, of respectable talents and attainments," says a late writer, "may be regarded as the representative of at least one thousand immortal beings to be moulded by his opinion and example."

Is there a demand for increased *contributions to objects of benevolence?* Arguments and appeals from pastors and returned missionaries may fail to call them forth. But they would not be withheld under a powerful work of grace. A close, penurious hand is not the companion of a heart that is full of love to God and man.

And is there an imperative necessity for more singleness of aim, and trustful, self-sacrificing, zealous endeavor, on the part of the respective members of Christ's body, for the saving of their dying fellow men? It would no longer exist, if primitive piety were but universally revived. When it prevailed, each disciple considered himself as called to the work of evangelizing the world, and went forth giving to it a practical illustration in his daily life. What is needful, then, save a return of the scenes of apostolic days, especially those of the ever memorable Pentecost? — a revival of the simplicity of purpose, — the entire consecration, — the scriptural faith, — the self-denial for Christ, — the earnestness and individualism of effort, so signally developed in the early triumphs of Christianity, when the multitude of them that believed were of one heart and one soul; neither said any of them that aught of the things which he possesses was his own, and "great grace was upon them all."

And *why may we not anticipate the return of Pentecostal seasons?* Why may not Christians *now* be "filled with the Holy Ghost," as were they in primitive times? Not for the working of miracles, it is true, but for the doing of "*greater works than these*," is the special presence of God's Spirit available still, for the disciples of Christ. Moreover, is there not left for our encouragement, the assurance of God's readiness to bestow that Spirit? Behold how the Saviour has condescended to reason the case with us! "If a son shall ask bread of any of you that is a father, will he give him a stone? or if he ask a fish, will he give him a serpent? or if he shall ask an egg, will he offer him a scorpion? If ye then, *being evil*, know how to give good gifts to your children, *how much more shall your heavenly Father give the Holy Spirit to them that ask him!*" Why, therefore, despairingly lament that Zion languishes? Why deplore the many defects in Christian character, and the worldliness and impiety that prevail, with no efforts toward their removal?

> "Whence do our mournful thoughts arise,
> And where 's our courage fled?"

God lives! He still watches over the interests of his

kingdom on earth. He waits to be gracious. He *will* hear prayer, and bestow his blessing.

Let ministers, then, be more earnest in their endeavors for *a general and powerful revival of primitive religion.* Let them cry aloud and spare not. Let them set the trumpet to the mouth, and rally the hosts to battle. Let them call upon the people to take to themselves words, and to return unto the Lord with mourning, and with fasting, and with supplication. Let there be weeping once more between the porch and the altar, and the cry heard, "Spare thy people, O Lord, and give not thine heritage to reproach, that the heathen should rule over them!" Let them preach, and labor, with special reference to more holiness, and deeper religious feeling, and greater engagedness. Let them expect revivals, and not rest satisfied without them. Let them act upon the suggestion of Edwards, and be *fellow-helpers* in the work, — often meeting together, and acting *in concert;* since, as he intimates, the very sight or appearance of a thoroughly engaged spirit, together with fearless courage, and unyielding resolution, would do much towards accomplishing the desired end.

And let believers generally strive after higher attainments in spiritual life. Let there be more of that weeping and confessing and praying and covenanting together, among Christians, which characterized the revivals of days gone by, and which always accompany, to a greater or less extent, the commencement of a powerful work of grace. Let the great theme be *salvation;* and the great aim the stirring up of each other's minds by way of remembrance; and the snatching of perishing souls from the everlasting burnings. Let any *one* believer who mourns over the desolations of Zion, not wait for the revival of the entire congregation, but personally take hold upon the promises, and, in the name of the Lord, resolve never to cease from efforts and prayers for increased religious interest, until it is experienced. What may not *one individual*, thoroughly in earnest, under God, accomplish!

Fellow Christian; *let the work begin in your own bosom!* Call upon the Lord to arouse your drowsy soul. Why stand you idle? The *future* is the time for rest, — the present for *action*. "In this theatre of man's life, it is reserved only for God and his angels to be lookers-on." Up, then, and seek to compass life's great end. Go *work* in the Lord's vineyard. He will soon call you to your account. The Judge standeth at the door. The throne will be set. The books will soon be opened, and men's destiny sealed up forever. "Behold, I come quickly; and my reward is with me, to give every man according as his work shall be."

Have you no spirit for his service? Is your heart cold, and dead? Then take it to Christ.

> "None but a bath of blood divine
> Can melt the flint away."

Repair again to Calvary, where your heart was first melted. You cannot linger amid the scenes of the crucifixion, and remain unaffected. The Pilgrim in his journey to the Celestial City, saw a *cross*, and stood still and wondered. He stood and looked, and looked again, "till the springs that were in his head, sent the waters down his cheeks." Draw near, that you may behold a suffering Jesus. Gaze upon that countenance that had borne no other look than that of benevolence. What *agony* is now depicted! Look again. See those hands, that had been filled only with benefits for men, — that had fed the hungry, opened blind eyes, and ministered healing mercies to the sick, — see them now pierced through with cruel nails! Look again. See those feet, that had borne him up and down, throughout the length and breadth of the land on errands of mercy, now spiked to the wood! And again. See that majestic brow, that had been ever radiant with more than a brother's compassion, — see it now all besprinkled and dripping with blood!

> "See from his head, his hands, his feet,
> Sorrow and love flow mingled down!"

Look, if you can, still once again. There is that *heart*, that throbbed with more than a *mother's* affection, — is it not enough that it has been crushed, till it can beat no more? No, it must *bleed!* See! they have pierced it with a spear! His *heart's blood* is pouring forth! And *for what? Wherefore* all this?

> "Was it for crimes that *I* had done,
> He groaned upon the tree?"

Yes, for YOU, my brother, *all this for you!* Surely must *such* love warm into life the best affections of your soul. Surely must it constrain you to make such returns as lie in your power, by putting forth every possible effort to save those for whom Christ died. And thus *yourself* revived, encourage this same spirit among your brethren; nor cease, at the mercy-seat of the Everlasting Father, to urge, with the faithful of the earth, the earnest cry, "O LORD, REVIVE THY WORK!"

END.

www.ingramcontent.com/pod-product-compliance
Lightning Source LLC
LaVergne TN
LVHW010242110826
845151LV00004B/1369
9781425524043